Robert Gay has truly gotten down to
as to why so many in the body of Christ today never ___,
realize the full potential of their destiny in God. This book is
a must for every pastor and every believer to read, study, and
devour. If this one principle can be rightly employed in the
life of the church it will literally propel us toward our God-
given destiny. This will be on the required reading list for all
my leaders and every member of my church for that matter.

—PASTORS TOM AND JANE HAMON
CHRISTIAN INTERNATIONAL FAMILY CHURCH

New apostolic leaders are emerging all across the body of
Christ with a fresh new word that the Spirit is speaking
to the churches. Very few of those leaders offer a word as
straightforward and foundational as the one Robert Gay has
been hearing. Thanks to his book, *Planted*, the Church can
hear and benefit from this incredible message from God.

Apostle Robert Gay is a pioneering voice among church
leaders who are taking a fresh look at old standards of the
Gospel. I'm grateful that *Planted* provides, not opinion, but
biblically based insights concerning what God expects of
His people—the key element for blessing and maturing the
saints. The message is simple, "Be planted in the house of
the Lord or fail to receive and achieve God's destiny provision for your life." I found it a wonderful affirmation for
what God is speaking to the Church. Excellent!

In the current apostolic reformation, his book is practical, concrete, and immediately applicable. I encourage you
to not only read it, but also to study, share, and apply it.
It is such a valuable tool that I recommend it to every one
of our pastors. I plan to make it required reading for all
our Network leaders and strongly suggested reading for the
whole church. I am very excited for it to be in print.

—DR. JIM DAVIS
CHRISTIAN INTERNATIONAL APOSTOLIC NETWORK
NETWORK DIRECTOR

Robert Gay is a pastor of a growing church and he is speaking in a world accustomed to rapid change, shallow commitments, and questionable priorities. This work addresses a critical problem common among all churches.

He begins with a solid explanation of his premise and quickly states the basic principles. Backed up by personal testimonies of those who sit under his ministry, he moves quickly to challenge and minister to the problems of shallow commitments, selfishness, pride, wrong priorities, offenses, cares of life, and all the excuses used to justify the "uprooting" of membership. Like a thoughtful and capable physician, he moves quickly from the problem to the solutions.

This work is well balanced. In a time when the Church is placing emphasis again on the empowerment of the saints, it would be good for the saints and leaders to read this.

—Dr. Kirby Clements
Ministerial Network Director,
Chapel Hill Harvester Church

Often, because of advanced technology, we find ourselves living in a world of increased isolation. The twenty-first-century Christian desperately needs true and practical revelation on "Covenant connectedness"—helping people understand the importance of meaningful relationships within the local church body. Robert Gay has birthed a powerful "now" word, which he has lived! *Planted* is required reading for every leader and every member of our church!

—Dr. Richard K. Perinchief
Apostolic Leader, Spirit Life Church
Ocala, Florida

I highly recommend this book as a tool among the gifts of five-fold ministry, and of the saints in the body of Christ. It will be a stabilizing force for all believers who follow the directives set forth in the pages of *Planted*.

—Dr. Henry Jones
President, IAM Harvest Network

PLANTED

ROBERT GAY

CREATION HOUSE
A STRANG COMPANY

PLANTED by Robert Gay
Published by Creation House
A Strang Company
600 Rinehart Road
Lake Mary, Florida 32746
www.creationhouse.com

Unless otherwise noted, Scripture quotations are from the New King James Version of the Bible. Copyright © 1979, 1980, 1982 by Thomas Nelson, Inc., publishers. Used by permission.

Word definitions from *Biblesoft's New Exhaustive Strong's Numbers and Concordance with Expanded Greek-Hebrew Dictionary*. © 1994, Biblesoft and International Bible Translators, Inc.

Cover design by Terry Clifton

Library of Congress Control Number: 2004112092
International Standard Book Number: 1-59185-661-2

05 06 07 08 — 9876543
Printed in the United States of America

ACKNOWLEDGMENTS

I WANT TO THANK the many wonderful people who have helped in the producing of this book. First of all, I want to thank my wife, Stacey, who has been my support and a source of strength for the twenty-three years we have been married. We have stood together and seen God do wonderful things as we have been faithful to Him. Thank you for being a faithful wife, mother, and pastor.

I also want to thank my three wonderful children, Joshua, Kayla, and Micah, who in their early years of childhood traveled with us as we ministered extensively. You have made your daddy and mama proud and we love you very much. It is such a delight to have all three of you laboring with us in ministry.

I want to thank my father and mother, R. L. and Wanda Gay. You have always been an inspiration and encouragement to me.

Thank you for teaching me the way of the Lord and just being there. Your support through the years has been invaluable.

To my spiritual father and mother in the Lord, Bishop and Mom Hamon, I want to thank you for your spiritual impartation into my family's lives and mine. We owe so much to you and your faithfulness to pioneer for others. You are truly reproducers of reproducers and those who have loved unconditionally. Thank you for standing with us.

To Pastor Tom and Jane Hamon, I am thankful for your kind words and inspirational attitude you have displayed for the seventeen years we have known you. We have learned so much from you both by precept and the example you have set. Thanks for your faithful friendship.

Last of all, I want to thank the leaders and congregation of High Praise Worship Center. God looked all throughout the world and sent the greatest people He could find to our church. You have been a great blessing to Stacey and me, and we appreciate how you have stood with us and supported us in the writing of this book. We treasure the relationship we have with each and every one of you. Thank you for being the experimental spiritual environment where the message of this book was preached, practiced, and proven. We are blessed to pastor such wonderful people.

CONTENTS

FOREWORD

BY DR. BILL HAMON

*R*OBERT GAY PRESENTS some of the most vital truths necessary for members of the Body of Christ to be fruitful and successful. Being raised on a farm, I fully understand the principles of sowing seeds and growing crops. Using the planting of plants in a field and the process they go through to fulfill their destiny of being fruitful is so applicable to Christ's commands to Christians to be fruitful.

There has been a spirit of independence and self-will prevalent within the church for the last few centuries. It has been like the description in the book of Judges of the children of Israel that everyone did that which was right in their own sight. Almost everyone became a law unto himself, unfaithful, and not committed nor subject to any leadership authority.

This book brings wisdom and scriptural truth about Christ's

attitude concerning members of the corporate Body of Christ being planted in a local church. Every pastor will appreciate this book and will want to give a copy to each of their members. Every saint of God should read this book with an open mind and a receiving heart.

The teachings of this book are in agreement with the book I wrote, called *The Day of the Saints.* Robert emphasizes that every saint has a ministry to fulfill, but must be planted in a local church to more effectively fulfill that ministry. In my book, *The Day of the Saints,* the emphasis is that every saint has a ministry to fulfill, therefore we can rightly declare that every saint is a minister.

During the first 200 years of the Church, the word *minister* was not used as a clergy title, but a word describing what saints do in their calling as members of the Body of Christ. Ephesians 4:11–16 declares emphatically that Christ's fivefold ascension gifts of apostle, prophet, evangelist, pastor, and teacher were given for the purpose of equipping the saints for the work of their membership ministries. Verse sixteen emphasizes that the body of Christ grows and increases as every member is actively functioning and fulfilling their part.

Though every saint is a ministering member, it does not mean that saints can be separated from the local church and be a law unto themselves. The local church is a representation of the corporate body of Christ around the world. I wrote in *The Day of the Saints* that "saints are to be the church 24/7, that is twenty-four hours a day, seven days a week. They are the church, and functioning church members in their workplace just as much as when they are inside the four walls of the local church." However, this in no way implies that saints do not need to be planted in a local church with commitment and faithfulness to the pastor and fellow members.

There is a desperate need for the truths found within this book to be made available to every Christian. I believe this book expresses what is near and dear to the heart of God for His Church.

Thanks, Robert, for learning these truths through revelation and life experience, and then sharing them with the rest of the Body of Christ. Many will be planted more fully and become fruitful in God's kingdom because of this book.

PREFACE

*T*HERE IS A great need in the body of Christ today for stability in the life of believers. As a pastor, I have found that those who will become planted in a local church have stability as a natural byproduct. When families begin to serve the Lord together in the local church, there is a quality God releases in their lives that can be received in no other way.

It seems that over the last several decades an attitude has crept into the church that de-emphasizes the importance of being committed to the house of the Lord. It minimizes the importance of being a part of a strong local church. The fruit of this attitude has negatively affected the lives of believers.

When I was young, my family went to church every Sunday. The thought of staying home was never a consideration. Sundays were dedicated and consecrated to be spent in church.

Not only did we go on Sunday mornings, but we went on Sunday and Wednesday evenings also. If we had special services, we were there. When I became a teenager, I attended the youth service at the church. Being in the house of the Lord was an integral part of my family life.

My childhood would be what most consider normal. I went to school and was involved in extracurricular activities. My father and mother were also involved in these things.

They were neither pastors nor ministers. They were simply faithful members of a local church who were volunteer Sunday school teachers. My father was a route salesman and my mother was a bookkeeper.

I played little league football and baseball. My father participated by coaching the teams. Yet, the house of the Lord (our local church) was still prioritized over our extracurricular activities.

My parents realized that going to church was family time. The local church contributed to the well-being of our family. It ministered to us. We were stronger because of what we received in the house of the Lord.

It seems as though there are many in the body of Christ today that have placed the Church, the gathering of believers, last on their list. No longer is it a priority in their lives. It takes a back seat to other things they have going on in their lives.

This trend has been excused by many as "changing times." I am not sure that the times have changed as much as hearts have changed. People have become more committed to themselves than the Lord. For some, pleasure has become what they desire more than being in church. Others have idolized their own feelings that have been hurt in some way or another.

I realize that everyone is busy. However, hasn't everyone always been busy? My father and mother both worked jobs that required at least forty hours a week. They participated with my brother and me in all of our extracurricular activities. Yet, because the church was a priority in our lives, we were faithful in our attendance.

We always have time to do what we want to do. People will make time to do what they really want to do. Could it be that some believers have allowed their love for the local church to grow cold? Could it be that we need God to come and revive our heart and passion for the church once again? Could it be that we need God to deliver us from selfishness that has crept into our lives?

Some today have become spiritual floaters. They go from church to church and never have a place where they become a vital part. God has a place for all of us. It is in that place that God will cause us to be fruitful and productive in the kingdom of God.

God's desire for every believer is that they be planted. To not attend church or move around from church to church is not God's will for our lives. We need to hear what God's Word says concerning the local church and its importance in the life of the believer. That is the primary purpose of this book.

My prayer for everyone is that they will allow the Spirit of the Lord to speak to them concerning their heart dedication to the house of the Lord. I believe we will commit ourselves anew as we see the promise and blessing that God has for those who will become planted in the house of the Lord.

I believe hearts will be changed. I ask the Lord to anoint our eyes to see, ears to hear, and hearts to understand and know that God has a destiny for our lives that is divinely connected to the local church. As we follow after that destiny, we will find greater fulfillment and please the heart of the Father.

Those who are planted in the house of the LORD shall flourish in the courts of our God.

They shall still bear fruit in old age; they shall be fresh and flourishing.

—PSALM 92:13–14

Chapter 1

GET SOMEWHERE
AND PLANT IT!

*A*S WE READ this passage of Scripture, we can see the desire and will of the Lord clearly stated. His desire is for His people to be *planted* in His house. God desires for His people to have roots in a particular local church.

The house of the Lord that the Psalmist refers to is a physical place of worship. The house of the Lord is the place where believers meet together. It is the place where we gather in order to praise and worship the Lord, be taught and instructed in the Word of God, and minister one to another. The house of the Lord is what we now refer to as the local church. God desires His people to be planted in a local church.

God's house is the fundamental place from which He reveals and exhibits His will and desire. The local church is the place God has chosen to reveal His character, nature, and heart. His house, the local church, is to be the representation of His personage in the earth manifesting His glory, power, love, and anointing.

PLANTED MEANS STATIONARY

The word *planted* conveys the meaning of being stationary or permanent. When something is planted, it does not move around. Something that is planted remains stationary. It is in a fixed location.

At times we may even say to our children, "Plant it." That means for them to get in a particular spot, sit down, and not move. I believe the Father is saying to His children today, "Get somewhere and plant it!"

For so long, in the body of Christ, we have had those who would bounce around from church to church. Many times we have referred to spiritual floaters as "church-hoppers" or "cruisamatics." They cruise around to all the churches in the city usually causing problems wherever they go. This is not the plan of God for any believer in the Body of Christ.

Many of these same Christians travel from conference to conference, but refuse to be planted. In their heart and mind, the wonderful conferences they attend substitute for being planted in a local church. Conferences and seminars are wonderful and can benefit believers immensely, but they should never substitute the local house of the Lord. If you replace the house of the Lord with conferences, you will miss out on much of what God has for you.

Some Christians have thrived on the food from televangelists, but have not had a local house of worship they called home. We must realize that staying at home and watching someone preach is not having church, nor does it signify that you are planted. We can appreciate and support television ministries, but it is not intended to take the place of the local church.

The Greek word for *church* is *Ekklesia*. It means "a calling out and assembly." You, by yourself, are a member of the body of Christ; but when the members assemble together, we have the church. Sitting at your house is not God's best for you. Since the church is "a calling out" or "the called-out ones," then know that God is calling you out of your house in order to be planted in His house.

PLANTING PRODUCES BREAKTHROUGH

The Scripture says those who are planted will flourish. The word *flourish* is defined as "to break forth as a bud." In other words—*breakthrough*! Those who are planted will have *breakthrough* in their lives. This is the promise of God that will be fulfilled as you allow His planting to transpire in your life. *Flourish* is also defined as "to blossom and to spread." Nothing blossoms without being planted. Planting is the prerequisite for the satisfying of God's promise.

As a pastor, I have counseled a number of people who have had varying problems and obstacles in their lives. The ones who had the greatest, and largest number, of obstacles in their lives have been those who had a history of not being planted.

I have come to believe that there are many obstacles that can be avoided by being planted in the house of the Lord. With being planted, there is protection, safety, encouragement, and blessing that come as you join a local church that teaches and preaches the Word of God.

The previous passage of Scripture also says of those who are planted, that they will be fresh and flourishing. (See Psalm 92:14.) These two words mean "rich, fertile, and prosperous." As a result of your being planted, there will be richness in your life that will cause fruitfulness and increase. You will be a productive individual excelling in all that you put your hand to. God's promise is abundance and prosperity for the man or woman who is planted.

Here is a testimony from a married couple who are members of our church in Florida.

> We became members of High Praise Worship Center in October 1999. We would come to services for awhile,

then stop for awhile, come for awhile, then stop for awhile. In March 2000, we had our home and vehicles repossessed from us. Our lives were total chaos! Both of us were sexually abused as children. My husband had a physical disorder and could not work. I lived in the land of "denial". We were at the place of signing divorce papers.

Pastor Robert began preaching on being "planted". We took it to heart and got planted in the church. Things began to change quickly. Our marriage was restored as we were set free and delivered. My husband was healed of his physical disorder and began working again. Things changed in every area of our lives. God began to perform miracles for us.

My doctor had wanted to do a total hysterectomy on me because my uterus was flipped and backwards. During a service at the church, I was prayed for by some of the leadership. As they were praying for me, I felt something flip inside my abdomen area (kind of like when you are pregnant and the baby kicks or moves). That flip was my uterus turning back over to its normal position. I went back to the doctor and he said there was nothing wrong with my uterus and I did not need surgery.

Also, our daughter broke her foot practicing dance. She broke the fifth metatarsal right off the bone. She had to wear a splint for two weeks until the swelling went down, then they would have to do surgery to fix it. We took her to church, where she received prayer. After 2½ weeks of wearing the splint, we took her to the orthopedic surgeon and he took another x-ray to make sure of the break and said there was nothing there. It was completely healed!

Later, we started our own business and became incorporated. We have now purchased a new van for the business, and my husband is working. We are experiencing family blessing, physical blessing, and financial blessing in our lives like never before.

Also, since we decided to get plugged in at church, we are participating in different areas of ministry. We have also been added to the prayer teams–the *faith* team! We thank God each and every day for our church! If it were not for being planted in the church, I do not even want to think about where we would be.

This testimony bears out the results of being planted in the house of the Lord. Getting planted brought stability into their lives. It produced the blessing of God that brought forth fruitfulness, increase, and breakthrough.

THE PERFECT CHURCH?

There are some who refuse to become a part of a local church (planted) because of the imperfections of the members. They want the church to be perfect and use the fact that it is not to excuse their disobedience to God's command. Imperfection in others is never a justification for not becoming a part of a local church and not being planted. You must realize that there is no such thing as the perfect church because it is made up of imperfect people.

Amazingly enough, the ones who expect the church to be flawless are the ones who have the character of Christ perfected in themselves the least (the most imperfect). Apparently, many people expect the church to be something that they themselves are not. It is like the man who looked for the perfect church and finally found it—it became imperfect the moment he joined. We must realize that the church is made up of imperfect people who have chosen to obey God and be planted.

And it shall be, when you come into the land which the LORD your God is giving you as an inheritance, and you possess it and dwell in it, that you shall take some of the

first of all the produce of the ground, which you shall
bring from your land that the LORD your God is giving
you, and put it in a basket and go to the place where the
LORD your God chooses to make His name abide.

—DEUTERONOMY 26:1–2

GOD DOES THE CHOOSING

Here we see a specific command for God's people to "go to the
place where the Lord your God chooses." The first thing I would
like to point out about this command is that God already has a
place He has chosen for us. There is a local church that God will
reveal to every believer to be planted in.

God knows exactly what we need to be able to grow and develop
spiritually. He knows much better than we do. Many times we think
we know what we need better than the Lord. However, Jesus said
that the "Father knows what you have need of before you ask Him"
(Matt. 6:8). If the Father knows what we have need of, then He
knows what local church we need. As we are planted in that place,
we will grow, mature, and develop spiritually. We must allow the
Spirit of God to lead us in our decision concerning where we are to
be planted. It will be to our benefit and save us from the heartache
and confusion produced by being in the wrong place.

The second thing I want to point out is that He does the choosing, not us. Living in a free country, we have become accustomed
to doing what we want to do, when we want to do it. We do not
want to submit our right to choose to anyone. We consider this one
of our fundamental rights. We have the blessings of liberty in this
nation coupled with the right to choose. We see this right given to
us in the Bible when Joshua stood up and said, "Choose this day
who you will serve." God gave His people the opportunity to make
the (right) choice. This did not mean God would still bless them
if they chose to not serve the Lord. He also gave them advice in
their decision-making process by telling them, "Choose life." There

is blessing or consequence involved in the choices that we make.

Similarly, as we see in this Scripture, the choice of where we go is not really ours. God makes that choice. After all, it is His house. He should be the one making the decisions. Our choice should be to agree with the will of God for our lives. The choice to obey will empower God's blessing. Remember the words of the prophet Samuel, "to obey is better than sacrifice" (1 Sam. 15:22).

THE SHOPPING LIST

It seems as though many people have a shopping list when they come to visit a local church for the first time. Although I believe that God can use the desires that He places in our heart to lead us, I have found that most of the lists that people arrive with are not necessarily God's desires. Most lists of requirements that people have for a local church involve convenience rather than commandment.

For example, a nursery ministry is not a commandment, but a convenience for the parents. Unfortunately, many make their decision based on the appearance, performance, and availability of a church nursery. Please understand, I think nursery ministry is wonderful. In our church we have nursery available for every service. However, our decision concerning where we attend church should not be based on things such as the nursery. Neither should it be based on children's ministry, youth ministry, length of service, or any other external condition.

In some situations, where these types of ministries are not available, God may be calling us (or those with the shopping list) to be planted there in order to assist that local church institute that particular ministry. Thank God for those whom God calls to aid in the pioneering process, otherwise there would be none of these ministries in any church today.

WHERE IS "THE PLACE"?

You may ask, "How do I find the place where God wants me to be planted?" Here are seven basic principles that will help you in locating the place where God wants you to be planted:

- The first and greatest principle is the witness of your spirit man. There will be a sensing and a knowing on the inside that you are with spiritual family. There will be a drawing of the Spirit of the Lord to that particular house of worship. You will have a sense of spiritual fulfillment and destiny.

    Inside of you, there will be a sense of peace and a perception that you are in the right place. It will be like a "green light" in your spirit man. The Bible says, "The spirit of man is the candle of the Lord" (Prov. 20:27). Our spiritual senses will reveal to us the plan and will of God for our lives, if we will be sensitive to them.

- The second principle is that you will be spiritually challenged to go beyond where you are presently. Will my faith be stirred to believe for greater than what I am presently experiencing? Is the pastor preaching the Word of God or "Readers Digest"? Do the messages that are delivered challenge me to go further in God, or does it pacify my flesh into a place of complacency?

    True pastors will challenge their congregation to reach further and higher. They will spend the bulk of their time encouraging believers to get out of their comfort zone rather than pacifying the spiritually lazy who want to go nowhere. Pastors who pacify the spiritually lazy create spiritual nursing homes. You are not called to retire, but refire!

- The third principle is that particular local church will be suitable for you and your family. The root word for *suitable* is *suit*. A good suit needs to fit correctly. You should be able to "fit and flow" with that particular body of believers. The apostle Paul said the church is "fitly joined together" (Eph. 4:16). The members in a local church should fit together. You should feel that you are an integral part of something that is not only positively affecting your life, but the lives of others also.

  Flowing with a local church means there will be an opportunity for your ministry to function. You need to ask yourself these questions: Will I be relegated to a pew warmer or will there be an opportunity for my gift to function? Is everything a "one-man show" or are there others involved in different areas of ministry? Will I be activated to function or put on reserve status indefinitely? I realize that there may not be an immediate answer for these questions. It also should be understood that this does not mean your gift will be able to be implemented instantaneously. There is a time of proving that needs to be observed. Yet, you can get some kind of inclination of these things by observing those around you. These are important questions to be answered.

- The fourth principle involved in locating where God has called you to be planted is this: You must be in agreement with the vision and direction of the church. The prophet Amos said that people cannot walk together unless they are in agreement with one another (Amos 3:3). If you cannot come into agreement with the vision, plan, and purpose of that particular house of the Lord, then you may need to look elsewhere. As a pastor, I have found the truth to be that those who are not in agreement with the church in vision, heart, and spirit usually cause problems in the church. I would rather those believers leave and find somewhere they can be in agreement if they cannot change their conviction.

There also needs to be some sense of doctrinal agreement. If there are major differences, there will be great difficulty involved in flowing with that particular local church. Your value system needs to be similar to that of the spirit and heart of the local church or you will find yourself conflicting on a regular basis.

Understand that this does not mean your doctrinal position will never be challenged by fresh revelation. Every historical move of God brought greater understanding and revelation than the previous. In God's progressive restoration of truth, our doctrinal positions will always be shifting to some degree as a result of spiritual illumination. However, to flow with a particular body of believers there must be doctrinal agreement on certain fundamental issues.

- The fifth principle is that you will be equipped, empowered, and motivated to do the will of God. Can you be equipped to do what God has called you to do and fulfill your destiny? Will you be empowered for works of service and be activated into your membership ministry? Are you motivated to arise out of a place of passivity and move forward?

In the first-century church, the word *minister* did not refer to a title of a clergy position, but to a service rendered by the believer. Every Saint has the calling, privilege, and power to minister the Holy Spirit, the Word of God, and graces of God to others. Every local church should be a congregation of ministers.

—Dr. Bill Hamon
The Day of the Saints (p. 30)

The ministry gifts of apostle, prophet, evangelist, pastor, and teacher are in the church for the purpose of equipping believers to fulfill their personal ministry. (See Ephesians 4:11–13.) Every believer has a God-given ministry and function in the Church and outside the Church. You must be in a place that is equipping, empowering, and motivating you to operate in your gifting.

- The sixth principle is that there will be spiritual food to eat. God does not want us to go to His house and not be fed. The place to which He calls us will be one of spiritual sustenance. You should leave spiritually full and satisfied as if you had been served a five course meal.

  Course one may be the fellowship with the other believers at the beginning of the service. Course two could possibly be the praise and worship as you are ministered to by the presence of the Lord. Course three would be the offering time where you are able to take great delight in giving to the house of the Lord. Course four should be the main course of the teaching and preaching of the meat of the Word of God that brings strength and nourishment to your spirit and soul. And as you know, meals are not complete without dessert. So as your last course, there is spiritual ministry at the end of the service where you are participating as one who is receiving or ministering the Spirit of the Lord to others.

My parents live close to my family and me. Occasionally, we will go visit with them to say hello and see how they are doing.

11

Invariably, when we go over, they want to feed us. They ask us, "Have you had dinner?" and "Can we 'fix' something for you?" Parents want to make sure their children have something to eat even if their "kids" are in their forties.

Likewise, pastors have a desire to "feed the flock." A loving pastor will serve up a spiritual meal for his congregation. He will work to ensure that those who are planted will be spiritually nourished. Like parents in the natural, when you come over to his house (the one he has been placed in charge of), he will want to feed you.

- The seventh and last principle in finding the place where God wants you to be planted is there will be a sense of belonging. God desires for us to be a part of a covenantal spiritual family. When you find "the place," you will begin to have a sense that you have come into the company of those of "like precious faith." You should not feel as though you are an alien from another planet. When people feel alienated they alienate themselves.

To remain planted in any local church you must have a sense of belonging. Every believer should have a group of people that they can relate to on a spiritual and social level. Those people make up the local church in which God has called them to be planted.

I realize in saying this, there are some who seemingly never feel as though they belong anywhere because of rejection issues within their lives. They feel rejected before anyone has been given a chance to reject them. This type of believer must get planted in a place where they can first of all get healed and delivered of their rejection. The spirit of rejection can destroy God-ordained relationships if we do not allow ourselves to be set free. The first step towards freedom from rejection is to get planted in a local church that has an understanding of deliverance and healing.

The decision you make concerning where you are to be planted cannot be made on the basis of personal convenience. It must be based upon the principles that govern the kingdom of God. These principles that have just been identified are all biblical principles that God has instituted. These are necessary to observe as factors in the choosing of the place God has called us to be planted.

I believe the Spirit of God desires to lead and guide us in the decision of the local church in which we are to be planted. God has a place that is just right for us and it will be exactly what we need in order to grow and mature in the Lord. He knows what type of ministry we need in order to be fruitful.

DIVINE CONNECTIONS

Many people today feel as though it does not matter where they go to church, just as long as they go. I can appreciate that, at least, they want to be in the house of the Lord. However, it is important to realize that God has an ordained place for every person to be. It is important to God that we are in that ordained place, not another. Divine connections happen when people are positioned correctly in the kingdom of God.

Playing football as a young boy, I learned that a team member being out of position could cause your team to lose. There are a lot of Christians today that are "getting beat" by the enemy because they are out of position. They are not properly and strategically planted where God desires them to be. Consequently, they suffer all kinds of loss in many areas of their life. Part of the solution for this dilemma is to get planted where God has chosen.

Several years ago, a family moved to our city from another state. They moved because they sensed the Lord was speaking to them to become a part of our church. They had just gone through a very traumatic experience in which they had been taken advantage of financially. As a result, they had to file for bankruptcy.

It was a very difficult experience for them. They had always been people of integrity and paid their bills. However, the situation was so grave that there was no other alternative for them. They ended up losing their house, their van, and many other personal belongings. They moved to our city with not much more than the clothes on their backs.

When they arrived at our church they were wounded. They were "shell-shocked" from what they had just walked through. To say they needed healing would be an understatement. As they shared with me what they had experienced and the struggles they were having, I counseled them to get planted and allow God to heal them and bring restoration. I assured them that God would restore what the enemy had stolen if they would commit themselves to the will and plan of God for their lives. They began to obey and carry out the counsel they received.

When they first moved, things were a bit uncomfortable for them. They had always lived in the same city where their extended family lived. Their children were now away from their grandparents. They were not accustomed to some of the ways that we functioned in our local church. They were challenged with finding new employment in a city that had not traditionally paid good wages. You could say they were being stretched.

Not long afterward, God began to perform miracles in their lives. Within a short period of time, they were given a new car. Not much longer following that event, they were given another new car. The Lord began to bring promotion to them on their jobs. She found employment at a medical office in the city. She was then promoted to the chief administrator over three different medical facilities. Likewise, he began to get promotions on his job as God brought advancement and increase.

Today, they are living in a new home they were able to purchase two years from the time they had filed for bankruptcy. They are making more money than they ever have in their lives. Their family is strong and their children are serving the Lord. They serve as part of the leadership team at our church and minister on a regular basis.

It is amazing what takes place in someone's life when they get planted. They persevered and pressed in to see the breakthrough they needed. It came as a result of them being planted in the house of the Lord and being positioned for blessing.

God has given us a command to be planted in the house of the Lord. He has a specific place that He desires for us to be. As we are planted, we will see the blessing of the Lord come into our lives and our families. God will cause us to develop, thrive, and flourish as we follow His direction.

But you shall seek the place where the LORD your God chooses, out of all your tribes, to put His name for His dwelling place; and there you shall go. There you shall take your burnt offerings, your sacrifices, your tithes, the heave offerings of your hand, your vowed offerings, your freewill offerings, and the firstborn of your herds and flocks. And there you shall eat before the LORD your God, and you shall rejoice in all to which you have put your hand, you and your households, in which the LORD your God has blessed you.

—DEUTERONOMY 12:5–7

Chapter 2

GO THERE, GIVE THERE, EAT THERE

E CAN CLEARLY see a threefold command that God issues His people—*go there, give there,* and *eat there.* The Word of God declares that the things written in the Old Testament were written for our example and admonition. (See 1 Corinthians 10:11.) The principles we see in this scripture are given so that we who are New Testament believers may also be admonished by them.

The first command is *go there.* God expects us to go where He plants us. That means He wants us to attend church regularly, not just when we feel like it or have nothing else to do. Going to church is to be a priority in the life of a believer.

Unfortunately, only a small percentage (less than half) of all Christians in the United States regularly attend church at least once a week. That means, on average Christians attend a church service approximately once every two to three weeks—this is dreadful! It is amazing that there are more churches than ever before which are more conveniently located, yet the average attendance is far less than what it should be. I believe this needs to be corrected. The first thing we must do is to make attending church a priority in our lives.

The majority of Christians are faithful to their place of employment. They have disciplined themselves to go to work on a daily basis even if they do not feel like it. Yet, when it comes to church attendance, they go when it is convenient. If it is going to require any effort for them to show up, they stay home. What does this say about our dedication to the Lord? What does this say about our commitment to the body of Christ? We need to closely examine our priorities and put Jesus back at the top.

I have heard Christians make this statement, "I love Jesus, but I am just not into going to church." The people who make this statement do not realize what they are actually saying. The apostle John illuminates where the problem lies.

> If someone says, "I love God," and hates his brother, he is a liar; for he who does not love his brother whom he has seen, how can he love God whom he has not seen?
> —1 JOHN 4:20

The principle we see the apostle John bearing out in this passage of Scripture is that you cannot truthfully say you love the Lord and at the same time hate or detest being with others in the church (your brothers or sisters in the Lord). You must realize the "brother" that John is referring to is a part of the church, and may I even suggest, the local church. You cannot love God and hate your brother at the same time. It is amazing how many believers actually detest the church—by which I am referring to the local church.

My friend, if you do not want to fellowship, communicate, and be with other members of the body of Christ, then there is a problem in your life. Ultimately, it means there is a despising, detesting, and hatred of other Christians—your brothers and sisters in the Lord.

The majority of people who have come to know the Lord received the gift of salvation in a local church. When they were first saved, they wanted to be with other Christians on a regular basis. I am sure you can remember when you first received the Lord and how there was a zeal and passion for the Lord, His house, and His people. This is called your "first love." Over the course of time, as the result of unfortunate incidents, many Christians allow their first love to grow cold. The same apostle John who penned the previous scripture also wrote the book of Revelation. By the Holy Spirit, he had some things to write about "first love."

> To the angel of the church of Ephesus write, "These things says He who holds the seven stars in His right hand, who walks in the midst of the seven golden lampstands: I know your works, your labor, your patience, and that you cannot bear those who are evil. And you have tested those who say they are apostles and are not, and have found them liars; and you have persevered and have patience, and have labored for My name's sake and have not become weary.
>
> Nevertheless I have this against you, that you have left your first love. Remember therefore from where you have fallen; repent and do the first works, or else I will come to you quickly and remove your lampstand from its place—unless you repent."
>
> —REVELATION 2:1–5

May I propose to you that your first love is that which you loved when you first received salvation and were born again? May I also propose that part of your "first love" is loving God's house, the local church? In this admonition to the angel of the church

21

at Ephesus, God commands to remember your first love and do again your first works. There needs to be revival of our passion and desire for the house of the Lord. It needs to burn within our heart as it did at the time when we were first saved.

Many today go to church only when it does not interfere with any of the extracurricular activities they have planned. God forbid that they should cut their regular weekends at the lake short so they can make it back in time for the church service. After all, they need family time.

I would like to propose this for you to consider. Since when has our pursuit of pleasure become more important than the house of the Lord? When did going to church become something that was counterproductive for our family? When did being in the house of the Lord become something that was not family time? It seems the whole line of thinking and premise upon which some have based their decisions is flawed.

There is a lie that has been propagated by the enemy that says, "Your family problems can be solved and avoided by having a lot of family recreation." Please understand that I am not against family recreation, vacations, or anything of the like. Although, when that becomes what you live for and it is more important than being in the house of the Lord, there is a major problem. I have personally witnessed the truth to be this—the families who are faithful to the house of the Lord are the ones who become stronger than any others.

I believe that going to the house of the Lord is wonderful family time. It is a time of family bonding. It is a time that our families are being made strong. It is a time that we worship the Lord together as a family. What greater family time can you have than being in the presence of the Lord together?

On the subject of pursuing pleasure and fun, allow me a moment to share an observation. There are those who have been in dire family and financial situations that needed a breakthrough. I have watched them be faithful to the house of the Lord with their attendance, worship, service, and tithe. As they continued to receive the Word and continued to give, God brought forth breakthrough. God blessed them so much that they had money to do things they had never been able to do before. They purchased a boat, a motor home, and started their own business.

Soon after, I noticed they were only showing up every other Sunday. No longer did they attend the midweek service because their business required too much of their time. The next thing that happened was their tithe diminished. It was not difficult for them to give the $100 tithe on the $1,000 they were making. However, now that they were making $10,000 in monthly income, they seemed to have greater difficulty writing out the check for $1,000 in tithe.

Little by little they stopped attending and eventually stopped giving. Their boat and other recreational activities became more important. After all, they were working sixty hours a week and they deserved a break. It was coincidental that the only time they could take a break was during the time church services were being conducted.

All of this was justified because God was prospering them and they needed the "family time" for "family bonding." This was a way they could "cast their care on the Lord." The pressures and stresses of life necessitated them getting away every weekend so they could "chill." "Chill" is exactly what they did as they lost their fire and passion for God.

Eventually this road led to them losing their children to addictive behavior. Their business went belly-up. "Pastor, we don't understand what happened," they said. Let me ask you this question: Do you see what happened?

Their priorities were out of order. They began to pursue money and pleasure more than God. They had time for everything except what was important. Their pursuit of things was greater than their pursuit of God.

I have questioned sometimes if this kind of believer needed to go back to making only $1,000 a month. It seemed as if they were more obedient and faithful, and their families were more unified, when they had less money.

Jesus said to seek first the kingdom of God and all these things would be added unto you. God said that when you begin prospering, "Do not forget the Lord" (Deut. 8:11).

> "Beware that you do not forget the LORD your God by not keeping His commandments, His judgments, and His statutes which I command you today, lest—when you have eaten and are full, and have built beautiful houses and dwell in them; and when your herds and your flocks multiply, and your silver and your gold are multiplied, and all that you have is multiplied; when your heart is lifted up, and you forget the LORD your God who brought you out of the land of Egypt, from the house of bondage. . . . then you say in your heart, 'My power and the might of my hand have gained me this wealth.' And you shall remember the LORD your God, for it is He who gives you power to get wealth, that He may establish His covenant which He swore to your fathers, as it is this day."
>
> —DEUTERONOMY 8:11–14, 17–18

Forgetting the Lord is a sure way to see an end to His blessing in our lives. How many times have we seen people forget the Lord once they see their prayers answered? Throughout the Old Testament, when God's people would cease to obey, they would be turned over to captivity. Those things were written for our example so we would not make the same mistakes.

I have seen this happen far too many times. The prosperity that God brings takes some people down a path of selfishness and self-gratification. This is not the fault of the blessing. The blessing has only given an opportunity for the heart to be revealed. Rain does not create a bad seed; it merely sprouts what is there. Money and prosperity do not make people self-centered. It only gives them the wherewithal to demonstrate it.

It is of great importance that we keep our hearts guarded against things that would distract us from the house of the Lord. Jesus talked about how the deceitfulness of riches and the lust of other things would cause the Word to not bear fruit in our lives. Be thankful to God for prosperity and blessing, but we cannot allow the blessing to distract us from the Blesser. Neither can we allow it to distract us from the Blesser's house.

> There you shall take your burnt offerings, your sacrifices, your tithes, the heave offerings of your hand, your vowed offerings, your freewill offerings, and the firstborn of your herds and flocks.
> —DEUTERONOMY 12:6

The second command is *give there*. God declares in Malachi 3:10 that we are to bring tithes and offerings to the house of the Lord. There is a blessing that God releases on those who tithe and give offerings. It is a fivefold blessing as follows:

1. The windows of heaven are opened, releasing great blessing.

2. The devourer is rebuked for our sake.

3. Fruitfulness.

4. Physical evidence of God's blessing.

5. You become a delightful (healed and prospered) land.

I think it is important to understand that when believers do not go to church, they do not give to the church. That is one reason it is important for believers to attend church. The first command is a prerequisite for the second.

A family began to come to our church several years ago. They were a nice family who loved the Lord. They did not have a strong local church that they were committed to, but began to feel the Lord speaking to them concerning becoming a part of our church body.

One of the first meetings that they came to was during a financial conference we were conducting. Our church accountant who teaches on biblical financial principles was ministering in the meeting. Several things that were said concerning personal responsibility upset and irritated the husband. He actually considered not returning to the church. After he and his wife talked over the situation, they decided to continue coming to the church.

When they began attending, they would have been classified as a low middle class family. They paid their bills, but lived in a lower echelon of society. They lived in a small mobile home and drove a beat up car. They were surviving, but not thriving.

As they continued coming to the church, they began to give generously. They brought their tithe and offering on a weekly basis. Joyful giving is what they demonstrated on a consistent basis. It became a lifestyle for them. Anytime the church doors were open, they were right there with their offering.

Immediately, God began to bring promotion in their lives. The husband received a promotion to a managerial position. His salary quadrupled in a matter of months. God granted him favor with his employer and blessed the work of his hands. The wife, who had not graduated from high school and had worked as a lunchroom attendant in a public elementary school, furthered her education and became a teacher's aid, which increased her salary.

They have now moved from their small singlewide mobile home into a 3,500 square foot executive home that sports twelve-foot ceilings throughout. They are now driving new automobiles.

Their family is serving the Lord together. God has brought great breakthrough in their lives.

They had a chance in the beginning stages to uproot themselves from where God wanted them to be, but they decided to continue to go where God had planted them. Not only did they go, but they continued to give. The end result was the blessing of God manifested in their lives. Praise God!

Not only are we to give our finances, but we are also commanded to bring the "sacrifice of praise." It declares in verse seven of the previous Scripture that we are to "rejoice in all to which you have put your hand" (Deut. 12:7). This means we are to come and give God thanks and praise for His goodness and prosperity that He has brought forth in our lives.

Hebrews defines the sacrifice of praise as being "the fruit of our lips giving thanks to His name" (Heb. 13:15). That is the reason Paul said that we are to "give thanks, for this is the will of God in Christ Jesus for you" (1 Thess. 5:18). God's desire and will for us is to gather together for the purpose of unified and corporate giving of thanks and praise. It is wonderful to have a lifestyle of praise, but equally there is the requirement of the corporate gathering for that purpose.

> Lift up your hands in the sanctuary and praise the LORD.
> —PSALM 134: 2

Notice the Psalmist says to bless the Lord "in the sanctuary." You cannot lift your hands in the sanctuary if you are not there. Attendance is the prerequisite for blessing the Lord in the sanctuary. I believe that every believer needs to adopt a lifestyle of continual praise. However, I equally believe that there is something that we experience and receive through corporate worship that can be gained in no other way. Having a lifestyle of praise enables our corporate praise to be more anointed and accomplish more of what God intends for it to achieve.

As we read in the Book of Revelation, we see how there is an innumerable company around the throne of God who are worshiping him with great enthusiasm (Rev. 19:1–10). There is not just one person, it is a multitude. The heavenly pattern we see demonstrated is saints gathering together to worship the Lord. It is necessary for us to come together as a unified body of believers, the local church, and give God glory, praise, and honor.

We also need to give of ourselves. We should find an area of ministry in our church and put our hand to the plow. We will take greater interest in the house of the Lord whenever we are doing something in it. God will also reward us for our faithfulness to serve Him. We will discuss in more detail this important area in a later chapter.

The third command we find is *eat there*. Spiritual food will be in the place where God plants you. Elijah was told to go to the Brook Cherith and there he would be sustained. Elijah could have gone anywhere else and starved because provision was only in that particular place.

The name *Cherith* has its root in the same Hebrew word that is translated *covenant*. God was figuratively saying to Elijah to go to the place of covenant for provision. We must understand that we need to belong to a covenantal spiritual family; believers who have joined themselves together for the pursuing of the purposes of God to see the fulfillment of their destinies. We are to participate in covenantal relationships with those of "like precious faith" who believe that God has brought them together for a common purpose and goal. It is in that place we will find the blessing of the Lord and the spiritual sustenance we need.

When you are planted where God desires for you to be, there will be supernatural provision for you. God will cause the leader of that local church to provide spiritual food that will be exactly what you need to be properly nourished. You must also understand that what you need may not be what you want.

As a father of three children, I realize that children do not enjoy eating broccoli as much as candy. Nevertheless, I cannot just feed them candy even if that is what they prefer. If I did, I would be harming them. Likewise, a pastor of a local church cannot just feed his congregation sweets. There must be a well-balanced spiritual meal provided which may include some things that are not as tasty.

There are some people who will get angry and throw a tantrum when served something they do not like. This is called immaturity. The fact is, what you like the least may be what you need the most.

Psalm 1 declares that God will cause us to lie down in green pastures. The Lord has a green pasture for all of us to be fed. However, it is probably not a field of green lollipops, but rather a field of spinach. Yes, God expects us to eat our spinach!

He also has a Brook Cherith for us, just like He did for Elijah. It is our responsibility to allow the Spirit of the Lord to reveal that place to us and then respond accordingly.

> Then there will be the place where the LORD your God chooses to make His name abide. There you shall bring all that I command you: your burnt offerings, your sacrifices, your tithes, the heave offerings of your hand, and all your choice offerings which you vow to the LORD. And you shall rejoice before the LORD your God, you and your sons and your daughters, your male and female servants, and the Levite who is within your gates, since he has no portion nor inheritance with you. Take heed to yourself that you do not offer your burnt offerings in every place that you see; but in the place which the LORD chooses, in one of your tribes, there you shall offer your burnt offerings, and there you shall do all that I command you.
> —DEUTERONOMY 12:11–14

God warns His people not to offer up their sacrifices just anywhere. God told them they were to go to the particular place that He had chosen for them, and there they were to offer up their sacrifices.

There are a lot of great local churches in the world today. It is likely that there are numerous great churches in your city. However, God declares that there would be "the place." He did not say a place, He said "the place." God has "the place" for you.

It may not be the biggest. It may not be the one that has the most dynamic preacher. It may not be the one that has the greatest music ministry or youth group. It may be the one that is lacking in some of these areas. We need to stop looking at Church as a place for us to sit and be "enter-tained," but rather, go where God leads us and "enter-in."

It is in "the place" that believers are to go, give, and eat. I am convinced that many people today do not fulfill their destiny because they are positioned incorrectly. They are going somewhere, giving somewhere, and eating somewhere that God did not choose for them.

The consequence is that they wander around in the wilderness their entire life never accomplishing the will of God. They go and are never satisfied. They give, yet see no return. They eat and are never full. This tragedy could be avoided if they were only in the right place.

There is an old saying—It's not what you know, but who you know. There is a lot of truth in this statement that affects every area of our lives. Many today are trying to lean on their own abilities and knowledge to get them ahead in life. God has designed us to need each other more than our own ability. If we are just trusting in our own ability and knowledge, we are "leaning to the arm of the flesh" (Jer. 17:5) and the outcome of that is the curse. If we first lean on our relationship with God and then others, we will find that greater fruit will be the outcome.

Connections are so important in the body of Christ. If I purchase an airline ticket to Chicago from Panama City, Florida, I will most likely have to go through Atlanta. It is in Atlanta that I will connect to another flight. The flight from where I live in Florida does not take me to Chicago. It takes me to my connecting flight—my connection. Likewise, it is in the house of the Lord that we will make our connection for our destiny.

We need each other to fulfill our own personal destiny. God uses other people to help us get where we need to be. If we are not in the right place at the right time, we will miss our connection. God wants to bring divine connections in our lives, but we will have to be positioned correctly for this to happen. We need to make a decision to be where God wants us and be planted there.

We must make a decision to go where God has called us to be and be committed. We should also give that which God expects and is requesting from us. Then we will be able to eat and partake of the spiritual food that He has prepared. As a result, we will become strong believers in the house of the Lord that will be able to minister His love and anointing.

The LORD God planted a garden eastward in Eden, and there He put the man whom He had formed.

—Genesis 2:8

Chapter 3

THE MASTER GARDENER

ONE PREMISE I believe every Christian would agree on is that God is the Master Gardener. When we consider that He created every living thing in the world, we understand the magnificence of His ability. We marvel at His creation and its beauty.

It is interesting to point out that after all God created, He planted a garden. It does not say He created a garden, but rather planted a garden. The question I would propose and answer is: Why did God plant a garden when He had the ability to create one? Why would He take the time to plant when He could have just spoken it into existence? The answer to this question can be found in the words of Jesus.

> Then He said, "What is the kingdom of God like? And to what shall I compare it? It is like a mustard seed, which a

> man took and put in his garden; and it grew and became a
> large tree, and the birds of the air nested in its branches."
> —LUKE 13:18–19

Jesus said the kingdom of God is like a seed. I believe God was demonstrating to Adam a principle that would apply to everything in the kingdom of God. In order for something to grow it must first be planted. Planting is necessitated for fruit to come forth.

God is an expert gardener. Many of the parables that Jesus taught involved the seed and planting. Obviously, God knows His gardening. Since He is such a wonderful gardener, we should listen to Him so that we who are called the "planting of the Lord" can grow, mature, and bear fruit.

The responsibility of a gardener is to enable the plants to grow and mature by providing the proper combination of soil, moisture, light, and fertilizer. Our Father is the Master Gardner and knows exactly what you need in order to produce the greatest fruit.

Expert gardeners know exactly what kind of soil each plant needs for optimum growth. A cactus must be planted in a different kind of soil and climate versus a red rose. If you plant a rose bush in the desert, it will die from insufficient moisture. If you plant a cactus in a rain forest, it will die from too much water.

God knows exactly what kind of soil you need to be planted in. It is in that type of soil that you will produce maximum fruit. It is in that type of soil that you will bloom and flourish the most. It may even be a soil type that you do not like as much as another. Yet, it will be what affects your life greater than anything else.

I can remember when my wife and I walked through a season of transition in the mid-1980s. God providentially directed us to become part of a church and ministry that He was using to spiritually pioneer the Prophetic Movement. When we first arrived, our oldest son was two years old and there was no nursery or children's ministry, because the local church was still in the pioneering process.

We had come from a church where there was a nursery and children's ministry with every service. Keeping a two year old through a two to three hour service was not comfortable. Yet, we knew that God had called us there. He had called us there because He desired for us to be a part of, and participate in, the Prophetic Movement. The only way that prophetic fruit could be produced was to be planted in prophetic soil.

There were times that it was uncomfortable. There were times that our flesh wanted to find different soil. Nevertheless, God, the Master Gardener, had planted us in the soil we needed to be able to bear the fruit He desired. The end result was that fruitful prophetic ministry was produced in our lives. This would not have happened if we had been just anywhere. We were in the soil that God had chosen for us.

Our oldest son, Joshua, who was two years old at that time, is now eighteen years old. He is on staff at the church that my wife (his mother) and I pioneered over seven years ago and are presently pastoring. He is the director of Television and Video Ministries, and plays the bass guitar on the worship team. Now he is being asked to instruct and to assist other churches in establishing video ministries.

The lack of a nursery when he was two did not negatively affect him. As a matter of fact, it probably did him good to be exposed to mature ministry and learn to sit still in church. It may have been a little uncomfortable for my wife and I, but it certainly had no adverse effects. We are seeing the blessings of being where God plants you manifested in our oldest son.

Also, our other two children are already working and serving in the church. Our daughter Kayla, who is fifteen years old, is responsible for our Kid Dance Ministry in the church. Our youngest son Micah, who is twelve years old, runs our video presentations and is one of our drummers on the worship team.

In everything they have been involved in, they have all excelled.

It has transpired not only in the church, but outside the church also. My friend, there are great dividends to be realized when we obey God and are planted where He tells us.

Gardeners understand that plants must have the correct combination of moisture and light in order to achieve maximum growth potential. If we can analogize the Holy Spirit as the moisture (water) and the revelation of God's Word as light, we will get a clearer understanding of this principle as it relates to us in the house of the Lord.

Not all plants need the same amount of moisture. Not all plants need the same amount of sunlight. Some plants cannot grow without an extreme amount of sunlight while others will die from the same. Some plants will die from an extreme amount of moisture while others will thrive from the same. God knows exactly what combination you need and will plant you in the place where you will receive it.

I have heard this phrase before, "All Word and no Spirit will make you dry up. All Spirit and no Word will make you blow up." There is an element of truth in those statements. You must have the right combination. God will be faithful to lead you to the place where you will get the correct combination, so that you will neither dry up nor blow up.

I want to emphasize the word *combination*. In no way is this to be interpreted that we can exclude one or the other. We need both Word and Spirit. The Bible says they are in agreement (1 John 5:7–8). The Spirit gives life and understanding to the Word, while the Word gives balance and order to the Spirit.

Again, this has nothing to do with personal preference as it relates to things in the Church. This is about what you need to be fruitful. God knows the type of plant you are and the type of conditions you need to be a viable plant in His garden.

Another thing to understand about gardeners is that they know exactly where each plant needs to be placed for the garden to look exceptional. Not only do we need to be in the right garden, but we need to be in the right place in the garden. God plants us in the place where we will bring maximum beauty to His garden.

There may be times that you do not relish your place in the body of Christ. You may feel as if you are meaningless and have no value because you are not in the limelight. Let me assure you that every plant in God's garden is important and valuable.

The ground cover is just as important as the prominent plant. The things in the background help produce the overall effect of a beautiful garden. The star of a movie would be nothing without a supporting cast. The movie would also be lifeless. Likewise, the plants in the background give life and vitality to the garden.

You do not have to be the prominent plant in the garden to be important. Regardless of the role you play, you are valuable. You must learn to be content with the garden you are in and the place that the Master Gardener has positioned you.

The interesting thing about God's plants is they have the ability to move themselves. Can you imagine if you went to the nursery and found the perfect plant to complete your garden? You paid $250 to purchase it. You took it home and planted it. You then positioned lights to shine on this plant in order to highlight its beauty.

After a long day of arranging everything in your garden, you looked outside with great joy and satisfaction as you beheld the beauty of your garden. You then went to bed with a great smile on your face at the ecstasy of knowing that your garden was finally complete. The next morning you awoke with great anticipation of looking outside at your beautiful garden, the envy of the neighborhood.

You opened the curtains and peered outside. The joy that you had was turned into amazement. Soon it was followed by the feeling of anger as you looked across the street to see your plant, yes the $250 plant, in your neighbor's garden.

I wonder if the heavenly Father does not feel like that sometimes.

He found us and bought us. However, the price He paid was much more than $250. He bought us with the blood of Jesus. He then plants us in His garden and positions us where He needs us to be. Yet, because we do not like the soil and climate conditions, we uproot ourselves and figuratively run across the street to get in a garden He has not ordained for us.

Then we wonder why there is no fruit in our lives. We wonder why all the things we have heard are not working for us. We begin to question if God really meant what He said. This happens as a result of us uprooting ourselves and planting ourselves in the wrong place. We become a rose in the desert. We wilt away as quickly as we arrive.

There is an old saying that "the grass is always greener on the other side." It is amazing to watch how cows will stick their necks through a wire fence to eat grass on the other side. The grass is actually the same. Yet, for some reason they think it is better than what they have directly beneath them to the point that they will put themselves in a vulnerable position just to eat that grass.

How often are believers putting themselves in a place where the enemy can take advantage of them because they are trying to eat in a pasture that is not theirs? They are trying to partake of food that, on the surface, looks better than what they have. It looks greener. It looks more appetizing. Yet, the only thing that they receive at the end of the day is a sore neck from the fence rubbing against it. We must learn to stay where we are planted and allow God to work in and through us there.

Expert gardeners understand the principle of seasons. The Psalmist spoke about the tree that was planted and how it would "bring forth its fruit in its season" (Ps. 1:3). There is a season that God has ordained for every plant to bring forth its fruit.

In the wintertime, my lawn, that is primarily centipede grass, goes dormant. Some people plant rye grass in the winter because it is made to grow in the winter season. During summer the rye will die, but in the winter it will become green. We need to understand that our season may not be at the same time of another person. We cannot allow ourselves to get discouraged when someone else is in their season of fruitfulness, and we are seemingly going through dormancy. Rejoice with them knowing that your season is on its way.

Many people will uproot themselves because they do not see the progress in their lives they expect. Unfortunately, this results in a spiritual miscarriage of what God is doing within their lives. They have to go around the mountain again because they cut short what God was attempting to do within them. Dr. Bill Hamon has always said, "God always makes the man before the ministry." Many people terminate the "making process" prematurely and cause it to have to be repeated all over again.

I have heard people say, "I just need a new start." They are dissatisfied with everything going on in their lives. In actuality, the Master Gardener is fertilizing them with organic fertilizer and they do not like the smell. Many times this fertilizer is applied through a sermon their pastor is delivering. It may even be a special meeting where an area of their life that needs a spiritual adjustment is being addressed. It is in this time that God is in the process of making that plant strong and viable. You may not like the smell, but it will produce great growth if you will only allow God to finish His work.

I have told people who find themselves in the situation where they are itching to move and "get out" that the only problem with moving is they have to take themselves along. In other words, it does not matter where you go, you will always be with you. You cannot escape yourself.

Many frustrations that plague believers are actually rooted in internal conflicts and struggles. We seem to always look for something or someone to blame for these internal conflicts that we are experiencing. Many people blame their spouse, children, parents, job, the city they are in, and of course, the church and the pastor.

The premise is if they were just somewhere else, if they had a different spouse, if they had a different pastor, if they had a different church, then everything would be different. All of their problems would fade into the sunset. That is the biggest lie of hell that anyone could possibly believe.

Moving is not the solution. Having a different spouse is not the solution. Just think about this: you are only compounding the problems in your life if you pursue any of these options. Going down any of these streets will only lead to disaster and heartache. For some reason, our solution for changing the circumstance we do not like is escapism. May God deliver us from this option that so many believers keep on the table.

Escapism is the antithesis of perseverance. We are commanded to have the fruit of perseverance in our lives. The apostle James said, "You have heard of the perseverance of Job and seen the end" (James 5:11). What was Job's end? God restored to him double what was taken away and stolen. As some preachers have so well said, "Double for your trouble." If you want the "double portion," you will have to persevere like Job. To receive God's best in your life, you must not give up!

If we will only persevere and do not relent in the midst of adversity, God will bring us out on the other side with more than we had before. If we give up, we get nothing but the memory of the adversity we partially endured. Just think about this for a moment; you have the memory of the hardship that you suffered, yet no breakthrough on the other side of it. Instead of having a testimony of how God brought you through in victory and triumph, you have the testimony of a quitter. The Word of God declares, "Thanks be to God who always leads us in triumph" (2 Cor. 2:14). You cannot triumph without something to triumph over. Only the ones who do not quit are able to have the testimony of triumph.

When people experience any type of adversity, they usually look around to find out who is causing it. Many times, regardless of whom it may or may not be, they want to physically relocate themselves. The supposition is they will have a different boss, a different job, a different city, a different house, a different church, a different pastor, and it will be the solution to their problem. The end result is the same song, second verse. It becomes another chapter that is a repetition of the previous one in the exact same book.

In 1993 a movie was released entitled *Groundhog Day*. The story follows a reporter who had been sent to do a story on the groundhog, Punxsutawney Phil, and the hoopla of Groundhog Day. As a result of a snow storm, the reporter is forced to stay overnight. When he wakes up the next morning, the previous day, Groundhog Day, begins to repeat itself once again. The day continues to repeat itself until the reporter's attitude and disposition changes. He continues to experience Groundhog Day until he is transformed.

So many believers today are living life like this reporter in the movie, *Groundhog Day*. They feel the solution to their problem is to escape when in fact they will continue to go around the same mountain until they themselves change. We must realize that external change does not in of itself bring solutions to our situations. A different church with a different pastor will not solve all of our problems. My friend, moving from place to place in an attempt to find resolutions is not the way to live as a member of the body of Christ.

God wants you to be planted where He has ordained, and persevere through the difficult times. Paul told Timothy to "Endure hardship as a good soldier of the Lord" (2 Tim. 2:3). God also wants us to have a good attitude while we are persevering. The Lord expects not only obedience, but also a willing heart. "If you are willing and obedient you will eat the good of the land" (Isa.1:19).

The divorce rate today is astronomical in this nation primarily because people will not persevere in their relationships. You cannot be someone who is "here today, gone tomorrow" and have successful relationships, spiritually or naturally. This kind of behavioral disposition promotes instability and flakiness in the church. To have covenantal relationships, you will have to learn and experience the meaning of perseverance.

It is time for us to get where God wants us in His garden and stay there. Do not compare yourself to the plants around you. Be who you are in the garden of God. Grow at the pace that God has ordered for you. Bear fruit in your season and be happy. Be content when the fruit has fallen off the tree and there are new buds that are in the process of being developed.

On the subject of moving to another church, I do realize that there may be a time that the Gardener decides to transplant a plant. However, understand that it is not every month or even every year that the gardener does so. I believe when it is time for someone to move, those in spiritual authority will bear witness and sense the same. There will be recognition that the growth of that plant has exceeded the ability of the garden to contain it. Even the other plants will recognize it.

Most believers, who decide to go to another church, do not go because God is moving them. It is usually because they got upset or offended by someone in the church; many times by the pastor. This is not the way to be transplanted. Offense and church splits are not God's idea of transplanting. These are abominable things that bring reproach on the body of Christ. We will deal with this in a later chapter in more detail.

Let me encourage you to stay where God has planted you and bear fruit there. God knows what He is doing. Realize that He will make sure you get the correct combination of light (illumination of the Word), moisture (spiritual ministry and presence of the Lord), and fertilizer (spiritual discipline and accountability). He is the Master Gardener, and He is taking good care of you. Be satisfied and content with this understanding.

The LORD God planted a garden eastward in Eden, and there He put the man whom He had formed. And out of the ground the LORD God made every tree grow that is pleasant to the sight and good for food. The tree of life was also in the midst of the garden.

—GENESIS 2:8–9

Chapter 4

THE PRINCIPLE
OF THE KINGDOM

*O*NE OF THE first things God did after creating man was to plant a garden for him. God assigned Adam the responsibility of overseeing the garden He had planted. I am sure it was beautiful and awesome in appearance. This garden was to be a source of food for Adam. It was also in that garden that God placed the tree of life.

Likewise, God plants believers, like seed, in the ground of a local church, or the house of the Lord. He then assigns a pastor the responsibility of cultivating the plants in that garden. That garden becomes a source of spiritual food and sustenance for all who are there. God also causes that garden to become a "tree of life." It becomes a life-giving place where those involved can partake.

> Then He said, "To what shall we liken the kingdom of
> God? Or with what parable shall we picture it? It is like
> a mustard seed which, when it is sown on the ground, is
> smaller than all the seeds on earth; but when it is sown, it
> grows up and becomes greater than all herbs, and shoots
> out large branches, so that the birds of the air may nest
> under its shade."
>
> —MARK 4:30–32

We must understand that the divine principle of the seed (plant-ing) is *the* principle that governs the entire kingdom of God. I did not say it is *a* principle that governs the kingdom; it is *the* principle. Everything God originates starts in seed form. Every seed has a destiny. It will produce the fruit or crop that it is designed to pro-duce if it is planted correctly. It also has power to reproduce itself.

In the previous passage of Scripture I would like to draw your attention to the words "when it is sown." We could also read it like this: "when it is planted." Seed can do nothing until it is planted in the soil. You can speak to seed and nothing will happen. You can pray over seed and nothing will happen. Why? Because God designed seed to produce by being planted.

It is really miraculous how seed works. The moment a seed is planted in the ground there are chain reactions that begin to hap-pen. The seed begins a process of germination that, given the right conditions—sunlight, warmth, minerals, and moisture—will end up producing something beneficial for mankind.

A seed not planted is unbeneficial because it is not producing something of value. What would you rather have, a watermelon seed or a watermelon? Unless you do not like watermelon, I am sure you would prefer the watermelon over the watermelon seed. We must have the seed, but it is not the seed that provides nour-ishment to our bodies. It is the fruit of the planted seed.

Again, that seed will do absolutely nothing until it is planted. Like-wise, we cannot produce anything until we are planted. Planting is the requirement for spiritual productivity. You cannot produce spiritual fruit without being planted in the proper soil.

Please understand that you, just like a seed, have destiny locked up within you already. An apple seed will produce an apple tree that will bring forth the fruit—more apples. It will not produce oranges. Its destiny is not programmed to do that. Likewise, you have been divinely programmed to fulfill a particular destiny that is in your spiritual DNA. You are destined to produce something that is life-giving if you will allow God to plant you.

After you are planted, the process of germination will begin in your life. You will begin to go through chain reactions. Change will begin to come in your life. You will begin to sprout at first. It may not seem like very much in the beginning stages, but remember this: the mighty oak tree started as an acorn.

Let me paraphrase the previous verse of scripture that will help articulate what Jesus said in modern English. The principle Jesus was declaring is this:

That which is least, once it is planted, becomes greater than all. (See Mark 4:30–32.)

This is the principle that the entire kingdom of God revolves around. God takes the small and makes them great. The early church apostles were not men of great prominence. They were not highly esteemed in the community. They were from varying occupations; most with little esteem. Yet, understand this: while Peter was fishing on his boat, he had the seed of an apostle inside him. He just had to be planted correctly.

Many times believers will say they have little or nothing to offer. They believe no one would benefit from their contribution to the body of Christ. The problem is this—they keep looking at themselves in seed form.

If we look at an apple seed, we do not see an apple tree. If we look at an orange seed, we do not see an orange tree. Yet every apple or orange tree began as a seed. There are no apple trees that began any other way. There are no orange trees that grew as a result of some magical formula that someone poured on the ground. All trees began as a small seed.

When an apple orchard farmer looks at apple seeds he sees apple trees. You may see yourself as seed, but the Master Gardener sees you as a tree. We must begin to get His vision and see our potential as we allow Him to plant us in His house. We must also be patient during the growth process and allow Him to cultivate, fertilize, and prune us.

Every seed has to go through a death to the old before new life can appear. Jesus said, "Unless seed dies it will not produce" (John 12:24, author's paraphrase). Sometimes, when God plants you in a church, you may not immediately be placed in ministry or a place of recognition. You may go through a dying process first. Let me encourage you. If you are in the process where your fleshly vision, plans, and ideas are dying, know that God will bring forth His life, productivity, and fruitfulness, if you remain planted.

Jesus said of the seed, that once it is sown (or planted), it grows up. There is such a need in the body of Christ today for believers to come into a place of maturity. Many believers remain spiritual babies solely because they will not be planted. They do not have a church that they attend regularly. Some attend sporadically, only to be offended and then leave to go somewhere else.

As a father of three wonderful children, I have had the joy of seeing and experiencing all the stages of child maturity. When children are young, they seem to be very touchy. We owned full-size customized vans when our children were growing up. At one time, we decided to downsize to a large luxury car. We took this car on a ten-hour trip. Three children, ages three, six, and nine, in one back seat was interesting and challenging. "He's touching me," is what we heard for ten hours. We had that car for less than six months and then went back to driving a van.

Children are touchy. It takes very little for them to get upset or offended. They are in the maturing process and have to be taught to progress beyond childish ways. The apostle Paul speaks of some of these ways in 1 Corinthians 13. He said that those who mature and walk in the fruit of love will not be touchy or resentful. Growing up causes people to put away these childish ways.

Understand that there are challenges at every stage of development. Parents have the challenge to maintain proper expectations for their children. You cannot expect a one year old to dress himself. At the same time, a ten year old should be potty trained and off the bottle.

Likewise, spiritual development has its challenges for everyone involved—each individual and the pastor. Everyone is growing together and at times things may be a little uncomfortable. Yet, let me encourage you to stay planted in the midst of the uncomfortable situations. The season will change and things will smooth out. Do not abort what God is doing in and through you by uprooting yourself because "he's touching me."

Growth is not something that happens overnight. It takes time. Dr. Bill Hamon has said, "We grow in grace, we don't leap there." Many people do not like the process of growth and eventually choose to uproot themselves. We must "allow patience to have her perfect (complete) work." If you get impatient, the work will not be completed and you will not reach the stage of full fruit productivity.

We have heard this terminology before: growing pains. Yes, there are some pains in growing. There are some uncomfortable situations during the growth process, but it will be worth it when the seed begins to bear fruit.

I can remember experiencing some mild pain in my legs during the years of my physical growth. Today, I would not exchange the growth I experienced for no pain. There is an old saying in sports—No pain, no gain. There are some times during the growth and developmental stages that your muscles may be a little achy. There are times that you may want to quit.

PLANTED

I remember playing football and saying to some of my teammates "I'm quitting tomorrow." I wanted to quit when things got difficult. The fact is we all do. Thank God I had a father who would not allow me to give in to the desire to quit. He told me, "Son, you must finish what you started." Later on, I received the Most Valuable Player Award. I never would have reached my potential if I would have quit. You will never reach your full potential if you quit.

Jesus said of the mustard seed that once it is planted and begins to grow, it "shoots out large branches" (Mark 4:32). I believe this speaks of expansion that God desires to be produced. It indicates that as we allow ourselves to be planted, and then allow the growth process to continue, our effectiveness will increase so that others can actually shade under our branches.

I believe this also speaks of the blessing of the Lord that will increase in our lives, as we remain planted. God's blessing will be so great within our lives that others will be able to receive from the overflow. The branches reach so far that they become a haven for others.

We must understand that to become great in the kingdom of God we must be planted and allow God's growth process to be expressed in our lives. Greatness is birthed from those who are willing to be sown. Greatness will not be birthed in our lives if we abort the growth process mid-stream. We must commit to God's plan, purpose, and ways in order to see the manifestation of His excellence.

In 1982, the pastor of the church that I attended relocated. He was also responsible for leading the praise and worship. I had been the pianist and was knowledgeable in music (with a music major from college), but I could not sing very well. My wife and I had been married for less than two years at that time. She had become bold enough to let me know that when I sang, it had an adverse effect on the atmosphere.

The new pastor of the church asked me to begin leading worship

52

at the church since there was no one else capable. I made him aware that I had never done anything like this, but I would be willing to try. I can remember my first experience leading praise and worship in that church. It was exasperating to me. It was very challenging playing the piano and singing at the same time. I constantly felt as though I was running out of breath.

I continued to work at leading worship even though I felt somewhat inadequate. God bless those people that had to hear me sing in those early years of my ministry. My pitch left a lot to be desired. Slowly but surely I improved my natural skill, while at the same time developing the spiritual anointing that God had placed within my life. I did not realize at the time I started leading praise and worship in 1982 that I had the potential of being an anointed worship leader and songwriter. I was just filling in until somebody better showed up.

As I remained faithful to my assignment, God brought increase. I began to write songs that blessed the congregation. My voice improved to where my tone and pitch were much more consistent. I learned how to be sensitive to the Spirit of the Lord and follow His leading during the worship time. There were limbs that began to spread in my life that were ministering to others in the church. We began to see fruitful ministry.

In June of 1989, seven years later, I was having dinner at home with my wife and our children. Stacey answered the phone and said in an excited but subdued tone, "Robert, it's Don Moen from Hosanna! Music and he wants to talk to you." With great anticipation I said, "Hello Don." Don then proceeded to tell me that they needed someone to lead worship on "Hosanna 28, Victor's Crown." There were already a couple of my songs on the project and they were going to put a couple of more on there if I was willing to be the worship leader.

I experienced a whole range of emotions in a very short amount of time. It ranged from glee to shock to apprehension. I wanted to say, "Do you realize who you are asking? I'm the guy who can't sing. I'm the man who got drafted into worship leading when I felt I was incapable."

I agreed to do so in utter disbelief at what had just transpired. After I told my wife, we jumped around our little two-bedroom townhouse that we were renting. At that time, to lead worship on an Integrity Music CD was a worship leader's dream! The following month, we conducted the live recording of "Victor's Crown" in Fort Walton Beach, Florida. Several of my songs recorded on that project went on to be songs that touched the nations of the world. The songs "No Other Name" and "On Bended Knee" were among these.

My friend, none of this could have happened had I not been planted. Remember the principle that Jesus declared: "That which is least, once it is planted, becomes greater than all" (Mark 4:30–32, author's paraphrase). When I started leading worship I felt like the least of all, but I was willing to be sown and planted. The result was promotion and fruitfulness that touched the entire body of Christ. If believers would only be willing to be planted and serve their spiritual leaders, they would begin to realize their destiny in a greater way.

I can with all truthfulness say today that I am doing nothing because I started out with great natural ability. Everything I am doing started as the result of me allowing myself to be planted in the place that God wanted me. If believers will get an understanding of this principle, it will revolutionize their lives. God is not looking for the great ones, He is looking for ones who are willing to be made great.

Many believers want to be a blessing to others, yet are not willing to go through the process. The process of becoming a large and mighty tree does not happen overnight. It takes years of nurturing. In God's process, you may even become what you do not realize you are. An acorn certainly does not look like an oak tree. However, the acorn is an oak tree in disguise that waits to be revealed until someone plants it in the ground.

You must realize that strong trees take time to grow. They do not sprout overnight. We live in an "add water and stir" world today, and patience is a virtue that frequently goes lacking. Impatience will cause negative ramifications in our lives.

The story Jesus told of the prodigal son is a prime example of this principle. The prodigal son demanded his inheritance. He got impatient with his father and insisted that he have what was due him. The father gave it to him. Unfortunately, he was not mature enough to know how to manage his inheritance. He had the potential of being a strong oak tree, but he was still an acorn. Thank God there was restoration available, but we must know that this is not God's best. He wants none of us wallowing with the pigs in the mud.

One of the worst things that can happen to anyone is to get ahead of his or her time. After planting a seed, you may want it to grow faster. You may even pray that it grows faster. However, God has locked up in that seed its own timetable. You cannot rush it. You can do things to stimulate its growth, but at the end of the day it is only going to mature at a certain rate, even with optimum conditions.

There are those in the church who get ahead of God's growth pattern for their lives. They try to be something that they have not yet become. Yes, God said they would be great in His kingdom. Yes, they are the type of seed and are in the growth process. However, they are not yet fully mature. They try to become a nesting place while their limbs lack the strength to support a nest. The end result is the nest crashes to the ground.

Let me encourage you to not get into a hurry. For years I believed that Jesus was going to come any day and that if I was going to do something for the Lord, I would have to hurry up. I have now been married and in full-time ministry for twenty-three years. When I was seventeen years old and knew I had been called into fivefold ministry, I did not know for sure if I was even going to have a chance to fulfill any of it since Jesus' return was so imminent.

Although Jesus will come back and we do not know the exact hour, we do not need to be in a hurry. If you are always in a hurry you are anxious, which God says is sin. My friend, God is not in a hurry. So why should you be? Work and labor, and grow and mature at the pace that God has set for you. As you do, you will see God's promotion come into your life in His time. You will be like the tree that is planted that brings forth its fruit in its season.

But this I say: He who sows sparingly will also reap sparingly, and he who sows bountifully will also reap bountifully.

—2 Corinthians 9:6

Chapter 5

THE LAW OF SOWING AND REAPING

*T*HERE HAVE BEEN numerous books written concerning the law of sowing and reaping by many wonderful men and women of God. Most of them have dealt with this spiritual law from the perspective of its relationship to finances. Rightfully so, since this passage of Scripture deals with financial giving. However, I would like to examine this principle from a little different perspective. I would like for us to see this truth from the perspective of our life being the seed, and the local church in which God desires us to be planted as the soil.

One of the things we learned while studying the law of sowing and reaping, was the principle of reciprocation. We learned that God would cause us to reap in the same measure that we sowed (planted). I would like for you to consider this: you will reap from a local church in direct proportion that you allow yourself to be planted.

If you are not reaping anything from the local church that you are in, then you may want to examine yourself. Ask yourself these questions: Am I committed to this house? Do I participate in what is going on? Do I attend on a regular basis? Have I grown complacent in pursuing my destiny? Have I substituted my own desire for God's plan? Am I a casual observer or fully committed? How you answer these questions will determine what you need to do next to correct the problem.

It is God's plan for you to reap spiritual benefits from the local church body in which you are planted. It is also in His plan for others in that body to reap spiritual benefits from you. All good relationships are based upon mutual benefit. For you to not benefit is improper, just as for others to not benefit from you!

Any marriage that is one-sided will be plagued with problems. Any relationship that permits only one person to benefit will certainly be challenging. We may tolerate it for a short time, but if it continues we will become angry and resentful and begin to feel taken advantage of. This is not a pleasant position to be in.

The principle Paul articulates is this: the greater the planting, the greater the reaping. The greater we will allow our roots to go down into the soil, the greater we will be able to receive from the nutrients and therefore grow and mature. Those who allow themselves to be planted greatly will be blessed to a greater degree.

I have heard people say, "Well, I'm not getting anything out of church, something must be wrong with the preacher." At the same time, I have heard others comment on what a blessing the worship, the teaching, and the ministry times were to them. I have come to this conclusion: it is the ones who sow themselves into the church that reap the greater measure. Those who do not sow themselves into the local church end up receiving very little.

They also become critical of everything that is going on. They criticize the praise and worship. It is either too loud or too long. They criticize the children's ministry. It is either too juvenile or too mature for their little darling. The teaching of the Word is always on a subject they do not appreciate. If you are teaching on redemption, then they want something more on Christian maturity and ministry. If you are teaching on Christian maturity and ministry, then you should be preaching about redemption. They are never happy.

These are the people who sow little and expect everything to be to their liking. It really does not matter what you do, they refuse to be happy. These are the ones who the Psalmist described as ones who "sit in the seat of the scornful."

> Blessed is the man who walks not in the counsel of the ungodly, nor stands in the path of sinners, nor sits in the seat of the scornful; but his delight is in the law of the LORD, and in His law he meditates day and night. He shall be like a tree planted by the rivers of water, that brings forth its fruit in its season, whose leaf also shall not wither; and whatever he does shall prosper.
>
> —PSALM 1:1–3

The man who is blessed is the one who does not sit in the seat of the scornful. Complaining and murmuring always brought about God's judgment. (See 1 Corinthians 10:10.) Thanksgiving would always produce God's blessing. Sitting in the seat of the scornful will cause us to not be planted. We can choose whichever we want, blessing or judgment, by what we do.

The above passage of scripture talks about the blessed man being one who does not walk in the counsel of the ungodly. It is the ungodly person that will tell you to stay home and not attend church. It is the ungodly man that will tell you to withhold your tithe and not give to the church. They will tell you "all those preachers want is money." If you listen to what they are saying, you will be running away from your blessing.

The Word of God commands us to ignore the counsel and advice of the ungodly. Why listen to someone who has none of God's Word at work in his or her life? Why listen to the man whose family is not serving God and his kids are on drugs? God told us this, "Don't listen to losers" (Psalm 1:1, author's paraphrase).

The writer of Hebrews told us to follow those who through faith and patience inherit the promises of God. (See Hebrews 6:12.) If we are to receive counsel from anyone, we should find someone who has God's blessing manifested in their life. Do not listen to someone who has nothing working for them unless you want to arrive at the same destination.

Can you imagine going to receive business counsel from a person who has filed for bankruptcy numerous times? That would be foolish. The only thing you may be able to derive from them is what not to do. If we are going to receive business counsel, we should find someone that has been successful.

Can you imagine going to receive marriage counseling from a person divorced nine times? I would be very concerned about the validity of the counsel that I might receive. Do not listen to someone who has not appropriated God's promise in their own life. Also, do not listen to a loser.

Why should anyone receive counsel from the ungodly? The Psalmist said that he is like the chaff that will be blown away in the wind. (See Psalm 1:4.) In other words, once adversity comes, his house is going to come crashing down. Unless you want your house to do the same, do not listen to the counsel of those who are not planted in the house of the Lord because their counsel will not bring God's blessing in your life.

The blessed man is also one who does not stand in the path of sinners. What is the path that sinners walk? You certainly do not see them filling the church pews on Sunday mornings. You certainly do not see them bringing ten percent of their income to the church. You do not see them volunteering for church projects that need to be done. God tells us not to go down that path.

> Do not enter the path of the wicked, and do not walk in the way of evil. Avoid it, do not travel on it; turn away from it and pass on. For they do not sleep unless they have done evil; and their sleep is taken away unless they make someone fall. For they eat the bread of wickedness, and drink the wine of violence. But the path of the just is like the shining sun, that shines ever brighter unto the perfect day.
>
> —PROVERBS 4:14–18

We see how the path of the wicked is one that God forbids believers to follow. The end of that path is violence and destruction. It is the wicked who refuse to be in Church. It is the wicked who refuse to obey God. Going down that path leads to nowhere. It is a road that ends suddenly and plunges into a ravine.

You do not have to look very far to see how the path of the wicked leads to destruction. We see on television those whom the world idolizes. For example, the rock star who has a television show about his family. Look at where his path has led. Both of his children have been in rehab. You cannot understand a word he is saying. He is a poster child for a buffoon.

The wicked path he chose led him and his family into addictive behavior. His children can barely put a sentence together without using a foul word. They shout out profanities to their parents. Are these the kind of children you want? I certainly do not.

On the other hand, the path of the righteous shines unto the perfect day. What is the path of the righteous? Where are the righteous on Sundays? They are in the house of the Lord. Let me propose that the path of the righteous starts at the doors of a local church. I realize that a church does not save you or make you righteous, but righteous people are planted in the house of the Lord.

I heard someone say one time, "We're just not church people. We're Christians, but we just don't like church." This is like a husband saying, "I'm not really interested in my wife. I'm married, but I just don't like her at all." Isn't that a wonderful pattern for the home? Believers who do not like the church are guilty of self-centeredness. Everything is about them. Many times, these same people have numerous family difficulties because they do not understand that they are not the center of the universe. Life is about giving and sowing yourself into the lives of others.

I have observed the lives of men and women of God who have successful families. Their families succeeded in part because they were involved in the house of the Lord. They were dedicated to the local church. They became leaders in the house of the Lord. They were committed to doing the will of God.

The path of the righteous is a path that leads to life. It is a path that leads to God's blessing. It is a path that will lead to healing and deliverance. It is a path that will lead to family unity.

You do not find too many people getting healed and delivered at the pool hall. You also do not find people getting delivered at the local nightclub. The only things you find them getting delivered of in those places is their money and their innocence. You will find healing and deliverance in the house of the Lord.

The blessed man was described by the Psalmist as one who meditates in the Word of God. He is one who gives himself to instruction and counsel. Where do you find the Word of God being taught and preached? If you answered, "My local church," you are right. I am not saying that this is the only place that the Word is being taught, but it is definitely the place to start.

There was a husband and wife that came to my office to receive marital counseling. The condition of their family was dreadful. They were on the brink of divorce, their kids were performing poorly in school, and they were sick and broke. It was not a pretty picture.

They had been members of our church for a short time, but were not faithful in their attendance. They would show up twice a month sometimes. The husband was confusing when he tried to communicate. He suffered from seizures and was on disability at an early age.

They had come to a place where they were in desperate need for help. My wife and I sat down together and began to counsel them. One of the first things that we shared with them is they must make attending church a priority within their lives. We also encouraged them to go through a program that we have available at our church called "Restoring the Foundations." They received our counsel and began to apply the principles that we laid out which included consistently being in the house of the Lord.

As they were faithful in their attendance and received ministry in our counseling program, things began to change in their lives. God restored their marriage. The children's grades began to improve. The husband was able to carry on a conversation without being confusing. God brought deliverance in their lives. This started as a result of them planting themselves to a greater degree, which brought about a greater reaping in their lives.

The story does not stop there. Today, he owns his own business that is prospering tremendously. Both of them are serving on one of our post-service ministry teams. They are now being used by the Lord to bring deliverance to others in the church. They have become productive individuals in the community and the church. The key that unlocked much of this breakthrough in their lives was the principle of the kingdom of God, the principle of planting. They experienced the blessing of the Lord because they planted themselves securely and drew nourishment from the soil.

> He shall be like a tree planted by the rivers of water, that brings forth its fruit in its season, whose leaf also shall not wither; and whatever he does shall prosper.
>
> —PSALM 1:3

The Psalmist described the blessed man as one who is planted. As you are securely planted, fruitfulness and prosperity will become your reward. You do not become planted because you are fruitful, rather you become fruitful because you are planted.

We see here a threefold blessing to those who are planted: the blessing of fruitfulness, the blessing of freshness and longevity (not withering), and the blessing of prosperity.

Jesus said the Father is glorified when we bear much fruit. God gets glory when His fruit is in our lives. But fruit will not be produced if you are not planted. The sequence goes something like this:

1. You get planted.
2. You become fruitful.
3. Your Father is glorified.

The simplicity of this principle is amazing. Farmers see this at work every day. They plant seed in a field. The seed grows as it is watered to produce a crop. The farmers harvest it to make a profit, and are happy.

God is a like a farmer. He has a field—His kingdom comprised of many local churches across the world. He has seed—His people that have been redeemed by the blood of Jesus. He plants the seed—calls His people to be a part of a local church body. Fruit begins to be produced—His people begin to grow and mature in manhood and ministry. He harvests the fruit—a platform is provided for ministry to begin to come forth in the lives of His people that positively affects the church and the world. The Father is glorified—the seed He planted has produced His desire and intent, and has caused Him great joy.

People who are not planted are like trees with no fruit. They have no fruit because they are unable to produce it. Their roots are exposed to everything except what they need in order to be productive. They need to be planted so the nutrients of the soil can nurture them and enable them to bear fruit. Instead, they are exposed to the harsh elements of the sun and wind. Soon the tree that needs to be planted has dried up and blown away.

Abide in Me, and I in you. As the branch cannot bear fruit of itself, unless it abides in the vine, neither can you, unless you abide in Me. I am the vine, you are the branches. He who abides in Me, and I in him, bears much fruit; for without Me you can do nothing. If anyone does not abide in Me, he is cast out as a branch and is withered; and they gather them and throw them into the fire, and they are burned. If you abide in Me, and My words abide in you, you will ask what you desire, and it shall be done for you. By this My Father is glorified, that you bear much fruit; so you will be My disciples.

—JOHN 15:4–8

Understand this principle: you cannot separate Jesus and His church. To abide in Him, you must abide (be planted) in His church. Jesus said that those who do not abide in Him (are not planted) would wither. Plants wither when they have been uprooted and have insufficient moisture. Withering is not a good thing. Withering can be avoided with proper care and nourishing.

How often have we seen Christians who are spiritually withered? They are weak and frail. They are those who wander in the wilderness. They never seem to be able to get ahead; they are always behind the curve. I would propose to you that these are the ones who are not properly planted.

When plants are properly planted and taken care of they will grow and not wither. Psalm 1 said of those who are planted that their leaf would not wither. If you are withering, then you must examine your planting status. Are you planted? Where are you planted? The promise is if you are planted, you will not wither.

The way to prevent withering is to get plenty of moisture and food from the soil and allow your roots to go deep. Deep roots enable plants to receive moisture even when there is no rain. Deep-rooted plants are also more difficult to transplant.

To have longevity in God's garden you must remain somewhere

long enough to have an effect. There are those today who when the
fruit begins to blossom are ready to go somewhere else. They begin
to think they are ready to move on when the season of fruitfulness
comes. Remember this: the longer you stay, the deeper your roots,
the greater the fruit.

God does not want you to be a flash in the pan. He does not
want you to be a one-hit-wonder. You may be able to seemingly
bear fruit in a quicker manner and the short-cut may seem appeal-
ing. However, let me appeal to you to get planted and allow God
to cultivate and develop you. This will result in the full fruit production He desires for your life.

No one likes a tree that bears no fruit, even if the fruit is only
the beauty it adds to an area. Jesus cursed the fig tree because
He expected to find figs and there was none. (See Mark 11:14.)
Jesus said the fruitless branch would be taken away and ultimately
thrown into the fire. We may not have a full understanding of all
that Jesus meant when He said "in the fire," but I do not think it
was a place of blessing. Regardless of what it exactly means, I do
not want to be one of those branches. We can all agree that "in the
fire" is not where we want to be.

The solution to stay out of the fire is to be fruitful. "How?" you
may ask. It starts by being planted. You then must remain planted
and allow the moisture and minerals to begin to seep into you.
Jesus said it this way, "Abide in me." Be in the house of the Lord.
Be in His presence. Be in His Word. "Where?" you may ask. It is
the local church where He has called you to be planted.

The Psalmist went on to say of the blessed man who was
planted, that whatever he did would prosper. God desires to prosper His people. It is not His plan for His people to be spiritually
or financially poor. Just as an earthly father desires to give good
things to his children, the Heavenly Father desires it even more.
To receive this into your life you must follow His plan, which
involves being planted.

The man or woman who will be planted will be promoted. You will not get a promotion at your place of employment if you do not stay there. Those who jump around from job to job are always low man on the ladder. Their hope is to find that place that will immediately put them at the top of the heap. Unfortunately, it rarely, if ever, occurs.

Most promotions come to those who have been around for a while. Those who have put their hand to the plow and been faithful are the ones who are in line first. The person who just got hired and has had five jobs in the last year will probably not be promoted.

Likewise, in the kingdom of God, it is those who are planted that God promotes. As a pastor, I will not place someone who has just come to the church in a position of authority. That is primarily because they have not had ample time to receive the heart, vision, and spirit of the house in which God has planted them. Their roots are still shallow.

It is amazing how many times I have had people come to me and say, "Pastor, I am with you and you can count on me." I never see them again. Maybe they were trying to tell me that they would be with me in spirit and I could count on them never being at church again. This is not what they communicated.

It is one thing to say you are committed. It is yet another to fulfill that commitment. Only the ones who are planted will walk out that commitment. For those who will, there will be blessing and prosperity.

We have found that those who make a commitment to the house of the Lord become blessed in all they do. Their family situations begin to change for the better. Restoration begins to be manifested as they seek the Lord. Their business begins to advance. Financial breakthroughs happen for them.

Recently, I was talking to a builder who was building houses for two of our members. He told me, "I want to come over and visit your church." He went on to say, "I've noticed that the folks in your church are prospering; you must be doing something right."

The temptation for any pastor would be to take credit for the advancement of their members. It is easy for a pastor to say, "It's my great preaching and the revelation that I have brought that has brought them increase." Great preaching is wonderful and necessary just like revelation of the Word of God. However, at the end of the day, if God were not at work within their lives, there would be no kind of good fruit to talk about.

This was the result of these members being planted. The ones this builder was speaking of were members who had been securely planted for many years in the church. The blessing in their lives was due to the fact that they had been willing and obedient in the observance of God's command. They had been planted in the house of the Lord.

If we will choose to be planted, we will have the same results. We will see God's fruitfulness, longevity, and prosperity manifested in our lives. We will reap the blessing of the Lord to the same degree that we allow ourselves to be planted. Remember the words of the apostle Paul, "He who sows [plants] sparingly will also reap sparingly, and he who sows [plants] bountifully will also reap bountifully" (2 Cor. 9:6).

The bountiful blessing belongs to those who plant themselves bountifully. I encourage you today to get planted so the blessing of the Lord will come forth in your life.

"The Spirit of the Lord GOD is upon Me, because the LORD has anointed Me to preach good tidings to the poor; He has sent Me to heal the brokenhearted, to proclaim liberty to the captives, and the opening of the prison to those who are bound; to proclaim the acceptable year of the LORD, and the day of vengeance of our God; to comfort all who mourn, to console those who mourn in Zion, to give them beauty for ashes, the oil of joy for mourning, the garment of praise for the spirit of heaviness; that they may be called trees of righteousness, the planting of the LORD, that He may be glorified."

—ISAIAH 61:1–3

Chapter 6

GOD IS GONNA SHAKE YOUR TREE

*I*N ORDER FOR God to be glorified, we must be planted. God gets glory when we are planted in the house of the Lord. The words "that He may be glorified" have an unusual meaning in this passage of Scripture. It is one Hebrew word meaning to shake a tree. God wants you to be a tree of righteousness that is planted so He can shake your tree. Trees are shaken so that the fruit will fall and be enjoyed. There is fruit that God desires to be manifested in your life, which will only be produced as you are planted.

We shared previously how the Father is glorified when we bear fruit. Once again, it is articulated in this passage of Scripture. You will notice what precedes God being glorified is believers becoming the planting of the Lord. God wants us to be trees of righteousness. Trees are not easily moved. They have a root system that spreads outward and downward.

My family and I live in Florida where we have experienced hurricanes. My oldest son was born during Hurricane Elena. While we were in the hospital during his birth, I looked outside and observed trees being blown by winds in excess of 100 miles per hour. The limbs were moving and swaying dramatically. Some of them looked as if they were being bent over to the ground.

The amazing thing is after the battering of the storm, it was as if nothing happened. The trees were still there, the limbs were still in place—they had weathered the storm. Had the trees not possessed a secure root system, they would have blown over and possibly away.

It is the root system that not only nourishes the tree but also gives it stability. Likewise, it is our root system that will give us stability. It will keep us from being blown from here to there. A root system begins the moment that you allow God to plant you.

The apostle Paul commanded us to be steadfast and immovable. (See 1 Corinthains 15:58.) We will not be immovable if we are not planted. The only way to weather any spiritual storm that may come is to be secured by a strong root system. Without roots we will not be able to survive any of the storms of life. We will suffer loss if we are not planted.

There is a great need in the body of Christ today for spiritual stability. Those who are living the roller coaster lifestyle become thorn bushes. They are like tumbleweed blowing across the desert. Their continual vacillation frustrates anyone who has any dealings with them.

We have all probably had our times of instability. We have all had our times when we have vacillated. We cannot "cry over spilt milk," but we can certainly do something about how we are conducting our lives now.

From experience and observation, I can tell you that unstable believers are usually the ones who are not planted. They are the ones who fluctuate between two opinions. They are double-minded concerning where they are supposed to be. They are moved by circumstances when it comes to their church atten-dance. The unfortunate outcome of this lifestyle is disastrous.

The first thing that believers must do is get somewhere and stay there. It is important to be where God wants you and then not move. Choose to be immovable. Choose to stay in the midst of the challenge. Choose to give when you do not feel like it. Choose to praise when things seem to be turned upside down. This is the beginning of spiritual stability.

Spiritual stability happens as a result of developing a consistent way of living that aligns with God's commands for our lives. This is the attitude we need to adapt. God says, "Go to church," so we go without excuses. God says "Give," so we give without exception. God says, "Eat," so we eat the spiritual food we are served without prejudice.

If you always have an escape clause and escape hatch you will never develop stability. You will find yourself using the escape hatch on a regular basis. There will always be an excuse to not attend church. There will always be an exception to your giv-ing. There will always be prejudices exercised as to what you will receive from the pastor's teaching.

Jesus told the parable about the sower. He said the sower sows the Word. He then gives four different types of soil in which the word is sown. One of the soil types is stony ground.

> These likewise are the ones sown on stony ground who, when they hear the word, immediately receive it with gladness; and they have no root in themselves, and so endure only for a time. Afterward, when tribulation or persecution arises for the word's sake, immediately they stumble.
>
> —MARK 4:16–17

Jesus refers to the stony ground as those who have no root in themselves. He is talking about people who have no root system,

those who are not planted. He is referring to those who go to conferences and get excited. They go to all the revivals in town and
get *fired up*. The only problem is they have no root system.

The end result is this—they stumble. The original King James
Version says, "they are offended" (Mark 4:17). These are the folks
who get upset because the pastor did not say hello to them. These
are the same ones who decide to leave the church when their
"sacred cow" gets slain during the pastor's message. They are those
who have no root.

There seem to be some Christians who have very little determination or perseverance. It takes very little to cause them to give
up or quit. To fulfill our destiny and God's purpose for our life, we
must be determined. We must have a root system that keeps us in
place through the storms of life. That root system begins by being
solidly planted in the house of the Lord.

One of the elders in our church is in the United States Air Force.
His entire family is a very valuable part of our ministry. They have
functioned in various capacities since the inception of our church.
They have been like pillars—constant, faithful, and committed.

Several years ago he received orders from the Air Force to leave
the area for an indefinite period of time. He and his wife sensed
this was not the plan of God for them. They believed that God had
planted them in our local church and it was not the plan nor will
of God for them to leave. Now I thank God for our military and
this nation, but unfortunately Uncle Sam does not normally seek
the mind of God when he decides to transfer someone.

They felt such a strong conviction about this that they began to
see if they could get their orders cancelled. Unfortunately, they
could not. There was only one other alternative for them, and that
was to resign from the military. He had been in the military for
sixteen years and lacked only four years until retirement. If he
resigned before twenty years of service, he would lose all of his
retirement benefits. My wife and I counseled him to do everything

within his power to stay in the military so that he could be afforded what he had worked diligently for. We also agreed with them in prayer for God to perform a miracle for them.

Being of the firm conviction that they were supposed to stay in our church, he rejected the assignment and resigned from active duty. They made a decision that they were going to stay and God would have to perform a miracle for them.

He began to apply for different jobs available in the military that would enable him to stay in the area and maintain his retirement benefits. Job after job came available, but he was rejected repeatedly. Finally, about a month before his date of termination, a job came through for him. As a result, he would be able to stay in the area and maintain all of his military benefits including retirement.

I think you can imagine how they began to rejoice, as did all the rest of the church at the news of this breakthrough. God had performed a miracle for their family. Now, they have purchased their first home, which they built themselves. God was faithful to them as they were faithful to Him.

The story does not stop there. They had a son who was twelve years old. They wanted to have another child and had been attempting since not long after his birth. For many years and month after month they had been faced with disappointment. Immediately after they made the commitment to stay, she became pregnant. Today they have a one-year-old baby girl along with their fourteen-year-old son (the built-in baby-sitter).

It was their root system that gave them stability during the times of shaking. It was their roots that caused them to be committed when it seemed as though it could possibly have a negative impact on them. The end result of this firm planting was God's blessing and promotion.

God does not want us to be those who are here today and gone tomorrow. He does not desire us to be the one-minute sensation. He wants us to be there for the "long haul."

When I was younger, it was difficult for me to understand some of these principles. As I matured, I realized it takes time for strong ministries to be cultivated and developed. It does not happen overnight. Weeds grow overnight, but trees do not.

It seems as though the greater the potential for growth, the slower and less obvious it is. Weeds seem as though they spring up out of nowhere. The tree seed you plant seems to take forever to sprout. Once it finally sprouts, the growth is so slow that it is hard to measure on a daily basis. I have seen weeds grow half a foot over night. I have come to the conclusion that I would rather progress at a little slower rate lest I become a weed rather than a tree.

Many times we get in a hurry. We need to realize, as was said before, that God is not in a hurry. Progress on His timetable, not the timetable of the flesh and your own human desire. It takes time for a solid root system to develop. If you get ahead of God and do not allow your root system to be developed properly, when tribulation and persecution come, you will stumble and fall. You will wilt and dry-rot.

Realize, a tree is never any stronger than its root system. For the growth upward that is seen, there must also be growth downward and outward from the roots. The laws of physics that God put into place dictate that the higher something is built, the greater the foundation must be in depth and breadth to prevent what is being built from toppling over.

Allow God to finish His foundational work in you. Prepare yourself for the long haul. I am in for the long haul. How about you?

"....That they may be called trees of righteousness, the planting of the LORD, that He may be glorified."
—ISAIAH 61:3

In verse three of this passage of Scripture, we see the words "that He may be glorified." We have already shared how Jesus said that the

Father is glorified when we bear fruit. We know that God desires for us to be fruit-producing trees so that He will receive glory.

As mentioned before, the word *glorified* has a somewhat unusual meaning. It is defined as "to shake a tree." With this definition we have an insight to this Scripture that I believe is enlightening. God wants us to be trees of righteousness (fruit-bearing trees) so that He can come and "shake" our tree.

Living in Florida, I have had the opportunity to drive through orange groves. As you look out over the multitude of orange trees, you see more oranges than can be counted. If a citrus grower attempted to hand pick every orange off his trees, he would have to hire so many people that it would be counterproductive. His harvesting costs would be far too high to provide a product that consumers could afford to purchase.

Orange growers have a piece of machinery, an orange picker, that attaches to the trunk of the tree and shakes it. As the tree is shaken, the fruit falls and is caught in a huge bin. As a result, much fruit can be harvested in a short amount of time with fewer employees. The result is lower cost and higher profit.

Likewise, God wants us to be solid trees that He can shake. As He begins to shake, the fruit begins to fall. The end result is low cost and high profit for the kingdom of God. Maybe we should examine ourselves and ask, "Are we low cost–high profit Christians or are we high cost–low profit Christians?" I hope we are the high profit kind.

If the orange picking machine was attached to a tree that did not have a solid root system, the tree would be uprooted and fall over. How many times have we seen believers fall over or lean after a little shaking came along? God just wanted some fruit. Yet, they got offended and started leaning.

The persecution that came was meant only to shake their tree in order to cause the fruit to be revealed, but instead caused the tree to lean. The tribulation that came was meant to cause the fruit to be displayed, but instead caused the tree to lean.

Remember this: if we are not standing upright, we are leaning. If our attitude is not right, we are leaning. If our disposition is not right, we are leaning. If our expression is not right, we are leaning. It is only a strong root system that will keep you from leaning. That root system starts with being planted in the house of the Lord.

> That they may be called trees of righteousness, the planting of the LORD, that He may be glorified. And they shall rebuild the old ruins, they shall raise up the former desolations, and they shall repair the ruined cities, the desolations of many generations.
>
> —ISAIAH 61:3–4

Here we see some of the fruit that God wants to receive from our lives. He wants to rebuild the old ruins. There are areas of our life that the enemy has left in ruins—areas that have long-standing problems.

I have always been a believer in declaring God's Word over every situation. However, confessing God's Word does not equate to the denial of your weakness or a long-standing situation. Ostrich Christianity produces imaginary fruit. Until you are willing to deal with the situation head-on, you will live in a land of fantasy.

God wants the fruit of truthfulness in our lives. Truthfulness will cause you to take an honest evaluation of your life. It will cause you to look at hidden areas that God wants to rebuild. The good things that have fallen down will be erected once again.

The areas of your life that may be in ruins will be rebuilt as you are planted in the house of the Lord and develop a strong root system. The places the enemy has come to steal and destroy will be constructed once again as we allow the Word of God and the ministry of the Holy Spirit to be received in our lives. This is the fruit of being planted and having a secure root system.

The prophet Isaiah goes on to say that you will raise up the former desolations. The word *desolations* means to stun, stupefy, devastate, and to grow numb. God is declaring His desire to activate and sensitize our spiritual senses. I would like to discuss this sensitizing as it pertains to several areas.

First of all, God wants to activate the gifts He has placed within us by releasing a greater sensitivity to the voice of His Spirit. We must realize that the Spirit of the Lord is not mute. He is still speaking today. He is speaking through those who have ears to hear what He is saying to the church. He has placed within each of us divine enablements. Jesus said that His sheep would hear His voice. If you are born again, then you have the ability to hear the voice of the Lord. God desires to "raise up" our sensitivity level to His voice.

There is also the issue of Christians being desensitized to any conviction. There are many Christians today who have overridden their conscience to the point that it is seared. They can sin and not feel any conviction. In their minds, there is very little that is black and white—it is all just different shades of gray.

It is the Lord's desire to renew our conscience. If we can sin and feel no conviction then we have reason to question whether we are saved. I recognize that is a bold statement and it goes against much of what has been taught in evangelical circles, but please realize I am not suggesting anyone doubt either their salvation or God's grace. However, if we can participate in sinful activity and feel no pricking of our conscience, then something is seriously wrong.

God desires some fruit of sensitivity in our lives. I find that being in the house of the Lord allows our conscience to be renewed and restored. Being in the presence of God allows the Spirit of the Lord to deal with issues in our lives. Being planted gives God an opportunity to raise up the former desolations.

The last fruit mentioned is the repairing of the ruined cities. The word *ruined* is defined as dry or drought. How many people do we know that are dry and thirsty? How many do we know who need a fresh word from the Lord that will rain on them and refresh them? God wants to use you and I to minister to them. This is fruit that God wants to bring forth in our lives.

God wants us to be a cup of fresh water to those who are around us. Jesus said that out of our bellies would flow rivers of living waters. Any area that goes without rain or water will die. Drought has totally destroyed and devastated nations. We have living water inside of us. Will we take the time and opportunity to let it flow forth to those who are thirsty? I believe that as we do, God will be pleased with the fruit He sees in our lives.

It is interesting to observe that these are all things we are to do as we allow God's anointing to work in our lives and we become trees of righteousness. God is coming to shake our tree. We must allow the fruit to fall and be harvested. However, this will only happen if we are planted with a strong and secure root system.

...and every branch that bears fruit He prunes, that it may bear more fruit.

—JOHN 15:2

Chapter 7

GOD'S PRUNING PROCESS

*P*RUNING—WHAT A WONDERFUL word. It is something that all gardeners have to do at certain seasons. There are seasons that the limbs have to be cut back, dead leaves must be removed, and bad fruit must be eliminated. Jesus talked about pruning.

> Every branch in Me that does not bear fruit He takes away; and every brach in me that bears fruit He prunes, that it may bear more fruit.
>
> —JOHN 15:2

Jesus says in this passage that pruning is a good thing. Pruning is necessary for the tree to bear more fruit. I believe that the desire of those who are planted in God's garden is to bear more fruit. Fruitfulness is what pleases the heart of the Father. The Father is glorified when we bear "much fruit."

In order for you to bear greater fruit there must be pruning. That which is dead must be eliminated. That which is contaminating must be cut away. That which is prohibiting greater fruit from coming forth must be done away with.

God prunes every plant that bears fruit. If you make a decision to be fruitful in the kingdom of God, you are guaranteeing that you will be pruned by the Lord. We have already mentioned that God is the Master Gardener. He is going to make sure that His garden is properly cared for. That means He will certainly prune His plants at the right season.

The interesting thing about God's garden is that He has co-gardeners to which He assigns the job of pruning. These co-gardeners are called the fivefold ministry. The apostle, prophet, evangelist, pastor, and teacher are those who co-labor with the Lord in His garden.

The Lord Jesus has given the fivefold ministry special tools to carry out His pruning. They are revelation knowledge, understanding of the Word, divine wisdom, spiritual insight, and the gifts of the Spirit. These ministry gifts are in the church so that the church will be fruitful and productive.

> And He Himself gave some to be apostles, some prophets, some evangelists, and some pastors and teachers, for the equipping of the saints for the work of ministry, for the edifying of the body of Christ.
> —EPHESIANS 4:11–12

The fivefold ministry gifts are not given to do the work of the ministry. They are given to equip believers to do the work of the ministry. Another way of saying this is that the fivefold ministry are to enable the believers to be fruitful in the kingdom of God.

When we need to be pruned, God will not show up at the foot

of our bed with pruning shears. He will use those in the fivefold ministry to bring instruction, correction, or reproof into our lives through teaching, counseling, or a direct word from the Lord. God will use the preaching, teaching and ministry of the Word to deal with issues in our lives. At times, we may feel the cutting of the Word as the two-edged sword slices off that which has been keeping us from being productive in the Kingdom. It may even sting a little bit, but the end result is greater fruitfulness.

If a plant had the ability to be mobile, it would probably run when it saw the gardener get the pruning shears. Thank God they cannot. So let me share a story with you.

As the season for pruning arrives, a gardener goes to his shed to retrieve his old trusty pruning shears. He has had these shears for many years and is an expert at pruning. He is very thrilled to have such wonderful plants in his garden. He takes great pride in the particular care that he administers to his plants.

After retrieving his shears, he makes his way to the garden. The plant realizes the pruning shears are for cutting off limbs. The gardener begins to delicately and meticulously sever certain limbs that need to be pruned. The plant is somewhat angry with the gardener for such an assault.

The limbs that the gardener begins to cut off are limbs that the plant is proud of. They are limbs the plant has been growing for quite some time. "Why doesn't the gardener appreciate these wonderful limbs that I have grown?" says the plant. "Why has he come at me with such a violent instrument?" "What have I done other than beautify his garden?" "Why is he angry with me?"

The plant does not understand that the gardener is doing this to enable greater growth. The plant does not perceive, at that moment, the importance of what the gardener is doing. Until...

Springtime comes and other limbs grow out farther than they have previously. The fruit increases greatly as a result of the pruning. That which was a hindrance to fruit production is gone. The plant is now more fruitful than ever.

This sounds like a nice little story that would end with "and they lived happily ever after." It is actually the reality of what happens when God begins to prune us. There is just one major difference—God's plants have the ability to be mobile, run from the pruning, and retaliate against the gardener.

No one likes to be cut on. When God begins to cut things off in our lives it can be a little uncomfortable. As God begins to deal with issues in our lives, our natural tendency is to run. We want to get away from what is "hurting" us. The bottom line is that pruning can be an uneasy process to go through.

Jesus was able to endure the cross "for the joy that was set before Him." It was not a pleasant thing to go to the cross. He had to keep His vision fixed on the prize that was set before him. He kept looking at you and I.

In order to endure the pruning of the Lord, we must fix our vision on the end result. That being, we will bear greater fruit. We will become more productive. God will be glorified to a greater degree. This will give us strength and hope as we go through the process.

Part of the pruning process involves chastening. Chastening will produce the fruit of righteousness if we will allow it.

> And you have forgotten the exhortation which speaks to you as to sons: 'My son, do not despise the chastening of the LORD, Nor be discouraged when you are rebuked by Him; For whom the LORD loves He chastens, And scourges every son whom He receives.' If you endure chastening, God deals with you as with sons; for what son is there whom a father does not chasten? But if you are without chastening, of which all have become partakers, then you are illegitimate and not sons. Furthermore, we have had human fathers who corrected us, and we paid them respect. Shall we not much more readily be

in subjection to the Father of spirits and live? For they
indeed for a few days chastened us as seemed best to
them, but He for our profit, that we may be partakers of
His holiness. Now no chastening seems to be joyful for
the present, but painful; nevertheless, afterward it yields
the peaceable fruit of righteousness to those who have
been trained by it.

—HEBREWS 12:5–11

I would like to point out several things in this passage of Scripture. One is that we are not to despise chastening. The word *chastening* is defined as tutelage or disciplinary correction. We are not
to reject correction. We are to receive it in our lives.

I have heard believers say and sing, "Lord, mold me and make
me what you want me to be." They sound very spiritual, yet when
the Molder and Maker come, they reject the correction that is
needed to bring the molding. Many times they reject it because
they did not like the package it came in. The fact that God was
using another human being to be His hand of correction did not fit
with their doctrinal persuasion, so they rejected it. Molding and
making do not happen without tutelage and correction.

When I was in school, my teachers would correct my papers
that I turned in to them. They corrected them to point out the
mistakes so I would be sure not to make the same mistakes again.
They would show me what I should have written, as opposed to
what I wrote.

This is called tutelage or teaching. Effective tutelage includes
correction. Without knowing what we have done wrong, we will
not know what to change. We will continue in the error of our
way if our mistakes are not pointed out to us.

God places spiritual leaders in our lives that have spiritual understanding and wisdom. These leaders are actually there to "watch
out for our souls" (Heb. 13:17). They have to give an account to the
Master Gardener for how they have watched over the plants that

He sent to their sector of the garden. They are given the responsibility of pruning in their designated area of God's garden.

These co-gardeners are there to bring tutelage and disciplinary correction. Many plants despise chastening, so they end up uprooting themselves and finding a garden where the co-gardener is "nicer" and has either lost his pruning shears or refuses to use them.

The unfortunate situation is this co-gardener has been less than a good steward. The result is the plant produces little or nothing. This is a tragic story, yet happens on a daily basis to believers that have great destiny, but are not willing to go through the process.

It is time for us to understand that pruning is not a bad thing. It is God's love that He is pouring out on us. This is His confidence in us; that we will produce greater fruit. A gardener would not waste his time with a plant he believed was unable to produce fruit.

The Word of God teaches us the principle of accountability. Every believer, regardless of position or title, should be accountable to at least one person. They should have at least one spiritually mature individual that they will allow to speak into their lives. Without this, we will become a law unto ourselves and end up in error.

The Bible teaches us that we must give an account for our lives. Accountability does not start once you die and go to heaven. It starts now while you are here on Earth. It is God's safety and protection for our lives.

> Obey those who rule over you, and be submissive, for they watch out for your souls, as those who must give account. Let them do so with joy and not with grief, for that would be unprofitable for you.
>
> —HEBREWS 13:17

Those who function as pastors in the body of Christ are given a biblical responsibility to watch out for the souls of those whom God has entrusted to them. They will be required to give an account unto God for that charge. It is necessary for a pastor to be able to speak into the lives of his congregation for that responsibility to be fulfilled. A pastor who cannot do this is handicapped and will fail at his task.

In the Church, the role of the pastor mostly has been defined as visiting the hospitals during the week, preaching on Sundays, and making the church grow numerically. As apostles and prophets are being restored in the Church, the role of the entire fivefold ministry is being redefined.

The primary goal of fivefold ministry is not to make the church grow numerically. It is to mature believers. That means believers must have their bottles taken away from them. Yes, that means no more milk. They must be potty trained. Yes, that means the fivefold ministry is not going to continue changing diapers.

I can understand helping someone along as a newborn babe in Christ. However, when we have people that have been saved for twenty years that still behave like spoiled little babies, then we have a problem. If they can only handle the milk of the Word and rudimental Christianity, then something is wrong.

The church at Corinth was a church full of immature believers. The apostle Paul wanted to feed them with meat, but they could not handle it. (See 1 Corinthians 3:2.) They were very spiritual, yet very immature because of carnality issues.

Part of the problem is that pastors have enabled this type of immaturity. By not confronting immature spiritual behavior, we have enabled believers to continue down this path. I have told the members of our church on numerous occasions that I will not change their spiritual diapers. If they are a new convert, I will baby them for a while. However, I expect them to grow up.

My oldest son is now nineteen years old. When he was a baby, my wife and I changed his diapers. We gave him his bottles. I would even baby talk to him. My wife and I would feed him baby food with a baby spoon.

Now he is a young man. If he asked me to give him a bottle today, my response would be, "You've got to be kidding me. Absolutely not!" I am also not going to carry on a conversation with him in baby talk. I am going to speak to him like a grown man. I am not going to open a jar of baby food and feed him with a baby spoon.

How many times have pastors figuratively talked to twenty year old saints with baby talk? How often have we enabled believers to stay in a state of immaturity by our low expectation?

There are leaders in the church today that are more interested in drawing a crowd than seeing believers mature. There is nothing wrong with drawing a crowd, but if that is a higher priority than seeing believers grow up and mature then things are out of order. True pastors have a genuine concern for the sheep. We must ask ourselves: are we more interested in the spiritual growth of the sheep or our image achieved through our sheep pen growing? If we are more interested in the spiritual development of the saints, God will add numerically to our churches.

One of the problems that we have in the area of accountability is there are many people who are not planted in the house of the Lord. So when the pastor confronts those individuals who are not truly planted, they leave the church. They may have been members on the roll, but they were not planted with their roots secure. They were spiritual babies that became offended when their fleshly issue was addressed.

A husband and wife in our church came to receive counsel from my wife and me. As we began to talk, we could quickly see that the wife had some issues that needed to be addressed before there would be any breakthrough.

My wife, Stacey, and I began to address the issues. These issues were dead limbs that were keeping her from having a fruitful marriage. She did not appreciate the fact that we brought out the pruning sheers at that time. She got angry. She was expecting us to straighten out her husband, when in fact she needed the bulk of attention. She did not mind the pruning sheers being taken out for her husband, but her limbs were not to be touched.

We dealt with the issues with her husband and he received it. She, on the other hand, was not happy. She ended up storming out of the meeting saying that she was leaving and would not be back—an obvious attempt to manipulate and control.

My wife and I called her to try to talk some sense into her. Her husband did also. Fortunately, it worked. She got over her offense, came back, and received counseling (more pruning), remained planted in the church, and allowed God to complete His work in her. Today they are happily married and are functioning in ministry together in our local church.

You can see from this account how the enemy attempts to get people to run and hide when the season for pruning arrives. In essence they run from that which will bring fruitfulness and blessing within their lives. Most do not mind if someone else gets cut on, but just not them. You can counsel someone else and they would be willing to help you by writing out a script as long as you say nothing to them.

There is an ungodly attitude that seems to prevail in the Church today. That attitude is, "Nobody tell me anything because I am free in Jesus and if I need anything He will tell me." What these individuals fail to realize is that one of the ways that God speaks is through pastors and leaders in the body of Christ. God will use men and women to speak His will and purpose into our lives. He will also use them to confront areas that need changing.

Some believers, when being confronted concerning long standing issues in their lives, want the issues to be swept under the carpet. Their idea is that it was not a big deal and besides God has forgiven them. The problem is, they keep falling into the same ditch. These kinds of situations need greater measures of accountability in place.

Their feeling is that we should just forgive, forget, and move on. Please understand that there is no problem with forgiving someone, but if they keep falling into the same ditch, they must have help in order to develop a new pattern in their life. One of the tools used to produce this is accountability. Forgiving and forgetting without accountability and responsibility lead to anarchy and lawlessness.

We have a thing going on called "Jump and Run Christianity." This is where believers, when confronted, decide they would rather run than face the music. They would rather move to another garden than have the Gardener prune them. They say that they are misunderstood. They declare that nobody loves them.

The problem with jumping and running is the issues in their lives do not change. The issues continue. These types of Christians will bounce around from church to church until they find a gardener that has stored away his pruning shears.

The solution to all these dilemmas that are plaguing the Church starts with being planted. Being planted will keep you from running away when the pruning shears come out. It will produce stability for you in the midst of every situation.

Believers must learn to be teachable. Being willing to listen to someone who has already been down the road we are traveling will keep us from hitting the potholes. It will save our soul from trouble.

As those who are planted, we must be submissive and do what we are told to do. We cannot afford to maintain an attitude of nobody tell me anything. We must learn to follow the directives of those whom God has placed in authority within our lives. Remember, "They watch out for our souls" (Heb. 13:17).

The Apostolic and Prophetic ministries are restoring divine government back to the church. It is bringing God's order and structure throughout the body of Christ. The governing order of God brings with it responsibility: responsibility for leaders and followers, responsibility for shepherds and sheep, and responsibility for gardeners and plants.

All plants in God's garden must be willing to allow the Lord to prune them. Not only should we allow it, but also welcome it. It is the pruning that will cause us to be fruitful. It is the pruning that will cause us to be productive in the kingdom of God. May God come as the Master Gardener in our lives and carry on His pruning process.

On Sunday, go to church. Yes, I know all excuses. I know that one can worship the Creator and dedicate oneself to good living in a grove of trees, or by a running brook, or in one's own house, just as well as in church. But I also know as a matter of cold fact that the average man does not thus worship or thus himself. If he stays away from church, he does not spend his time in good works or lofty meditation. He looks over the colored supplement of the newspaper, he yawns, and finally seeks relief from the mental vacuity of isolation. [1]

—THEODORE ROOSEVELT

Chapter 8

WHAT IT MEANS TO
BE PLANTED

*I*N ORDER TO be planted in the house of the Lord we have certain responsibilities. These responsibilities are clearly articulated in the Word of God, and when followed will cause good fruit to come in our lives. One of the first responsibilities we have is very simple, yet is the one I have found is overlooked the most. It is the most basic requirement of being planted in the house of the Lord. That requirement is *go to church.*

> And let us consider one another in order to stir up love and good works, not forsaking the assembling of ourselves together, as is the manner of some, but exhorting one another, and so much the more as you see the Day approaching.
>
> —HEBREWS 10:24–25

I realize you can be a born again, Spirit-filled Christian and not attend church regularly. I know that going to the house of the Lord does not make you saved anymore than going to a shuttle launch makes you an astronaut. However, as born again Christians, we should desire to be in the house of the Lord. We should want to be around other believers. Something on the inside of us is amiss if we do not have a desire for the house of the Lord.

You can be saved and not attend or be a part of a local church. The end result is that you will miss out on the benefits of membership. Yes, there are benefits to being planted. Many have already been articulated. I believe the worst thing about not being a part of, and "plugged in" to, a local church is that you are sinning. Yes, I said sinning.

We are commanded in the Bible to be planted. The writer of Hebrews commands those who are redeemed to not forsake assembling together. In other words he was saying, "Do not stay home on Sunday mornings." That is my modern day interpretation of the principle he expressed. To stay at home and not attend Church when you have the power to do so is rebellious behavior. It is rebellion against God's word, which is sin. Here is an account from a member of our church in Florida.

> I could count on one hand the times I had been in a church as a youth. I was born again at nineteen. Two years later in fear and trepidation, I finally committed to obey God's command to not forsake the assembling of yourselves together. I did not know anyone at this church and I did not know what to expect, but it was there that I found a place to belong. I found brothers and sisters that I had more in common with than my earthly family. We had the same goals, we spoke the same language and we cared about the same things.
>
> I found a group of people who were working toward a common goal to promote and expand the kingdom of

God. I found my eternal purpose while being planted in a local church.

It is also through faithful membership in a church where iron will sharpen iron. Day by day and service by service, I have had the rough edges worn off of my personality, motivation, character, and morals. I was not just there for the good times to have my ears tickled. When I became planted, I heard the whole counsel of God.

I have found that it is when I became firmly rooted in a local body that I began the journey of being molded and shaped into the image of Jesus. I am grateful to be a work in progress for His glory.

I have had people come to me and say, "You know, I don't have to attend church to be saved." I thought to myself, "You are right, but saved people attend church." This is like a husband going to his wife and saying, "Honey, I don't have to live with you to be married to you and love you." I think we all realize that a man does not have to live with his wife to be married to her. However, they should live together because they are married.

There are people in the body of Christ today that are building their lives on a false premise. Their lives are like a house of cards that will fall down at the least little touch. They feel that as a Christian, they have little to no responsibility when it comes to the gathering of the believers.

What these people do not realize though, it is selfish for any believer to live only for him or herself and not consider others. These types of Christians are only concerned about themselves as the previous passage of Scripture bears out. It says to "consider one another" (Heb. 10:24). It is the self-centered that are only concerned about what they (their flesh) want to do. They are not concerned about the welfare of others and therefore do not "consider one another," but rather stay home on a regular basis.

This has been a problem in the church since the days of its

inception. The writer of Hebrews says, "not forsaking the assembling of ourselves together as is the manner of some" (Heb. 10:25). This was obviously a problem in the early church. People were staying home during the time that was set aside for them to be in the house of the Lord. They were "holy-rollers." The wake-up call came, they rolled over, and went back to sleep.

It is time for us to begin to prioritize the gathering of the believers together. If our lives are too busy for us to attend church, then we are too busy. We need to change some things about our life. We need God to come and order our steps and change our lifestyle. Going to church is important to the Lord, so we must make it important.

Again, the Scripture says that we are to "consider one another" (Heb. 10:24). We cannot do that at home in front of our television set. It does not matter if we are watching the best ministry in the world, we still have no ability to obey the command while we are at our house.

To bring a little greater understanding of this we will define the word *consider*. It is defined as to behold, observe fully, and discover. First of all, we cannot behold someone if we are not in their presence to see them. The only way to observe someone fully is to be in his or her company. We must spend some time with that person. To discover what another believer has to offer the body of Christ, we must be near them.

Columbus discovered America because he got into a ship and began looking. To discover those in the house of the Lord we must get into our ship (automobile) and go looking (drive to church). We will not be able to observe anyone in the church while we sit at home watching our favorite television minister. Television ministry is wonderful, but it is not a substitute for being in the house of the Lord.

We need to understand that by ourselves we are members of the body of Christ, but when we come together we become the church. We become the Ekklesia. We become the assembly of the saints.

You, by yourself, are a member of the body of Christ, but when the members assemble together we have the church. We should not allow ourselves to just be members of the body of Christ when God calls us to be a part of the assembly of the saints.

The apostle tells us to not forsake the *assembling* together. (See Hebrews 10:25.) That word *assembling* literally means "a complete collection" and "to collect upon the same place." If we are not at church, then there is not a complete collection. If we stay at home, then we do not collect upon the same place. If everybody stays home, we are all in different places. We are commanded to gather together at the "same place." He is talking about a literal physical location where a worship service is held.

You can make all the excuses in the world for why you cannot attend church. The enemy will even supply a few for you if you cannot come up with one yourself. The reality at the end of the day is this: your excuse will not excuse you. Jesus gave this parable:

> Now when one of those who sat at the table with Him heard these things, he said to Him, "Blessed is he who shall eat bread in the kingdom of God!" Then He said to him, "A certain man gave a great supper and invited many, and sent his servant at supper time to say to those who were invited, 'Come, for all things are now ready.' But they all with one accord began to make excuses. The first said to him, 'I have bought a piece of ground, and I must go and see it. I ask you to have me excused.' And another said, 'I have bought five yoke of oxen, and I am going to test them. I ask you to have me excused.' Still another said, 'I have married a wife, and therefore I cannot come.'....Then the master said to the servant, 'Go out into the highways and hedges, and compel them to come in, that my house may be filled. For I say to you that none of those men who were invited shall taste my supper.'"
>
> —LUKE 14:15–20, 23–24

It appears from this parable that the art of making excuses has changed very little since the turn of time. People still make the same excuses. "I've got a business deal going on." "I was just exhausted." Isn't that one creative? Why not just say, "What I was doing yesterday was more important." I am sure the Lord would be impressed with that one.

The giving of excuses is an art that has been perfected over the years. It is amazing how believers can become experts at giving excuses. The excuses are not really much different. They are just coming out of different vessels.

Remember what an excuse is. It is a legitimate reason that keeps you from doing what is of greater importance. All these men who made excuses had legitimate reasons why they could not come. The problem was in the value placed upon the invitation and the value placed on the one who invited them.

God has given us an invitation to be in His house. He tells us to come and not forsake the assembling of ourselves together. Many people respond appropriately and come to partake of the feast. Others disdain the invitation and place little value on it. The unfortunate thing in this whole scenario is that the one who did the inviting is insulted.

There are a lot of people today who are unintentionally insulting the Father God. He has given the invitation to every believer to "Come to My house." Most people would never think about saying anything to grieve the heart of the Lord. The thought of them insulting God and making Him angry is far from them. However, with their unwillingness to properly respond to the Father's invitation, they do insult Him. May God forgive and show mercy to us for the times we have insulted Him by our disobedience to His invitation and call.

This is not meant to condemn anyone. My prayer is that we will realize what we are doing when we refuse to go to the house of the Lord. Let us use this as an opportunity to take an honest examination of ourselves. Are we allowing other things to get in the way of our being in the house of the Lord? Are we despising God's invitation to come to His house?

The Greek word that is translated "assembling" is *episunagoge*. It is where we get our word *synagogue*. The synagogue was a regular gathering place for the people of God. It was on the Sabbath day in the synagogue that Jesus took the Book of Isaiah and read. It is interesting to note that Jesus did not sporadically go to the synagogue.

> So He came to Nazareth, where He had been brought up. And as His custom was, He went into the synagogue on the Sabbath day, and stood up to read.
>
> —LUKE 4:16

Notice it says that it was Jesus' custom to go the synagogue. That means it was His habit. He did it every Sabbath. He was not a twice a month attendee. He was faithful in His attendance. He was not a spiritual floater—Jesus was planted!

What is interesting about Jesus' faithfulness to the synagogue is that He was not in agreement with the teachers of the law. He would later refer to them as hypocrites, snakes, and whitewashed tombs. Regardless, Jesus still had a commitment to be in the house of the Lord.

I have heard people say, "All the churches in my city have no anointing, so I just stay home and have church by myself." I understand there may be a season where believers might have difficulty locating exactly where God wants them to be. I also understand there are some places that may not fit your spiritual taste. However, if Jesus could go to church and tolerate the teachers of the law and their powerless preaching, you can certainly overlook some weaknesses of the church in which He wants to plant you.

Too often believers are using what I refer to as "spiritual excuses." "I don't go because I'm at home praying." "I don't go because the Lord told me to stay home and study the Word." "There is no flow of the anointing so I'm better just to stay home." These excuses do not excuse us from the invitation that God has given.

If anyone could have had an excuse (and may I venture to say a reason) to not attend the regular services at the synagogue, Jesus could have. However, He did not. He was there every Sabbath. It was His custom. Jesus had a habit of attending church.

Do you want to be like Jesus? Then go to church!

The Bible says Jesus learned obedience through the things He suffered. I am sure there were times He was suffering on the inside hearing some of the teachers of the law. You have to remember; He was the Word. He had to listen to things that were possibly rubbing Him the wrong way. He had to listen to religious teaching that was infused with the traditions of men. I am sure He had to "bite His tongue" at times.

Jesus held His peace until it was His time. He kept silent until the Father released Him into His ministry. He honored the authority that was in the synagogue until it was time for His authority to be revealed.

Even though Jesus did not agree with everything the religious leaders were doing and saying, He was still there. I am sure that with all the good He may have received, He also learned what not to do. This can be just as beneficial to us many times.

Not only was it the custom of Jesus to attend church on a weekly basis, but also of the apostle Paul.

> Now when they had passed through Amphipolis and Apollonia, they came to Thessalonica, where there was a synagogue of the Jews. Then Paul, as his custom was, went in to them, and for three Sabbaths reasoned with them from the Scriptures.
>
> —ACTS 17:1–2

Once again we see the word *custom,* which means "prescribed by habit or law." It was Paul's habit, as prescribed by the law, to go to church. Paul obviously realized that the fourth commandment, "Remember the Sabbath day, to keep it holy," was still relevant for believers in the New Testament.

It is interesting to note that the Jewish synagogue was not a Christian church. It was the closest thing to it and a place where Paul would first have an opportunity to preach the Gospel. On the other hand, this also represented the people by whom he had been persecuted severely. So why would Paul go there?

I am sure Paul used his heritage and expertise in the law to open the door for him to be able to share in the synagogues. Ironically, he was not in agreement with the teaching of Jewish law. Neither was he in agreement with the doctrine of circumcision. Yet, he would go preach in the Jewish synagogue on the Sabbath when there was not an established Christian church.

This meant he had to frequent the synagogues because he was responsible for starting most of the churches in the cities he visited. You could begin to question if Paul had a death wish.

Why would Paul go to the synagogue on the Sabbath when he himself said that he was an apostle to the Gentiles? He said that he was not sent to the Jews but to the Gentiles to preach the Gospel of Jesus Christ. While there could be much speculation as to why Paul went to the synagogue, what we see expressed in the Bible is that he went because it was his custom.

Paul realized and demonstrated the importance of being in the house of the Lord. If there was not a New Testament church in town then he made the Jewish synagogue one by going there and preaching the Gospel. Paul had an understanding of taking dominion. Wow!

Jesus and Paul demonstrated the importance of being in the house of the Lord. They both demonstrated the principle of being planted. As we follow their example, we will see fruitful ministry in the kingdom of God.

Remember the Sabbath day, to keep it holy.

—Exodus 20:8

Chapter 9

REMEMBER THE SABBATH DAY

*O*NE OF THE commandments God spoke to Moses, in what we have referred to as the Ten Commandments, is to keep the Sabbath Day holy unto the Lord. I believe this commandment is still relevant for believers in the church today. It is a commandment that has *not* passed away with the introduction of grace, just as "Thou shall not steal" has not passed away.

We are commanded to keep the Sabbath (a seventh) day consecrated to the Lord. There is to be an intermission from our regular work for the purposes of the Lord. In both the Old and New Testament we can readily observe how God's covenant people would gather together on the Sabbath for the purpose of worship, teaching, ministry, and fellowship. There is no indication in the Bible that this pattern was to change, starting in the 21st Century.

PLANTED

In other words, this is still God's commandment for us that we are to follow today.

I would like to deal with several different issues that keep believers from observing this commandment or that causes them to minimize its importance in their lives. God did not give us this covenantal command for no reason. There is divine purpose that is linked to divine destiny for us as individuals and that of the corporate Body of Christ. As we understand these principles, we will be propelled into the fulfilling of God's will for our lives.

Let's begin by defining exactly where the Sabbath originated. Some would try to argue that the Sabbath began with the introduction of the Law, but that is not accurate.

> And on the seventh day God ended His work which He had done, and He rested on the seventh day from all His work which He had done. Then God blessed the seventh day and sanctified it, because in it He rested from all His work which God had created and made.
> —GENESIS 2:2–3

As you read this passage of Scripture, it can clearly be seen that the Sabbath originated at the time of creation. It did not originate at the time of the giving of the Law. *Sabbath* means "to desist from exertion," speaking more specifically of labor and toil. God paused to take a break on the seventh day. He ceased from His labor in order to rest and be refreshed.

In doing so, God left a pattern that we were to follow throughout the days of our existence here on earth. This was not something that was done with no forethought or spiritual significance. God deliberately took a day off in order to example that which you and I should be participating in today. He then at a later time, when the Law was given, felt it so important that He made it a commandment.

The word *holy* means "to sanctify, consecrate, and set apart."

God has commanded His covenant people to set the seventh day apart and consecrate it for His kingdom purpose. The Sabbath was designed by Almighty God at the time of creation to be an opportunity for man to be refreshed both naturally and spiritually. It was designed to be a day where those of like precious faith congregated together for His divine purpose.

When God said for His people to "Remember the Sabbath Day," He literally meant to remember. The word *remember* means "to recall." God gave an instruction to His covenant people to bring to the forefront of their thinking that which He instituted at creation. The commandment that He was giving was not something new. It was a principle that was already in operation before the Law was given.

> Six days shall work be done, but the seventh day is a Sabbath of solemn rest, a holy convocation.
> —LEVITICUS 23:3

The word *convocation* means a public meeting. This Hebrew word is also translated as *assemblies*. The Sabbath was to be a day set apart for the people of God to meet publicly at a certain place of assembly. *God designed it that way!* This was not my plan, nor am I saying this only because I am a pastor. This is God's design.

There are some who have accused local church pastors of only being interested in the growth of their local church. They feel that the exhortation of being in the house of the Lord is meant only to provide the preacher with someone to preach to.

Let me respond to that false assumption by saying that pastors have the God-given responsibility to preach and teach the Word of God. This includes the commandment for believers to gather together and be in the house of the Lord.

We must understand that pastors have been delegated a business. That business is to teach, preach, and proclaim that which God's Word says and motivate those who have ears to hear and obey. Pastors should tell their congregation members of their God-given responsibility to the local church.

There are yet others in the Church who feel that the commandment to keep the Sabbath day holy is an outdated commandment that does not fit with the current trends of our culture. They say that the pace of life today does not allow for the fulfilling of this commandment. They go on to declare that it is impossible for them to honor the Lord in this manner because of other responsibilities of life. I will attempt to address each one of these as best as I can.

We must first realize that God's Word does not change according to the current trends of our culture. God's Word is forever settled in heaven. (See Psalm 119:89.) If you begin going down that path, you are headed for danger. It leads to a life philosophy called situational ethics that determines right and wrong behavior only by the circumstance that one encounters. It is a lie from the enemy that causes people, including believers, to take a path that leads to all manner of sin and self-destruction. If we relegate interpretation of the Word of God to cultural trends at a given moment, we are guilty of the sin of Balaam. He compromised his integrity by opening the door of temptation and coveting money and acceptance.

Another realization that we must come to is that our pace of life should be determined by God's command and not our external desires and influences. To say that our pace of life is too busy is to idolize our own endeavors. It places our own thing above God's thing. By doing so, we have broken the first commandment which is "You shall have no other gods before me" (Exod. 20:3). If we say our own business is in the way of us fulfilling God's commandment, then we have placed our own undertakings before the Lord. This is idolatry.

I understand that we all have responsibilities. Life is filled with them. It is good that we take responsibility for our lives and become productive individuals. God commands us to be productive and fruitful. However, the responsibilities of life are not intended to supersede the commandment of the Lord.

Jesus spoke of the person who allowed the cares of life to choke the Word. There are many believers who are allowing their responsibilities (cares of life) to choke out the Word to the point that they no longer obey what it says. The end result of this lifestyle is fruitlessness. We must not allow our "busy-ness" to keep us from fulfilling God's command of keeping the Sabbath Day holy.

On the other hand, God's command was never imposed for the purpose of burdening us with obligation nor putting us in bondage to the point of not being able to "lift a finger" on the Sabbath. Remember that there is a ditch on each side of the road. Let's see what Jesus had to say about the Sabbath.

> Now it happened that He went through the grainfields on the Sabbath; and as they went His disciples began to pluck the heads of grain. And the Pharisees said to Him, "Look, why do they do what is not lawful on the Sabbath?" But He said to them, "Have you never read what David did when he was in need and hungry, he and those with him: how he went into the house of God in the days of Abiathar the high priest, and ate the showbread, which is not lawful to eat, except for the priests, and also gave some to those who were with him?" And He said to them, "The Sabbath was made for man, and not man for the Sabbath. Therefore the Son of Man is also Lord of the Sabbath."
>
> —MARK 2:23–28

The Pharisees were always looking for something whereby they could make accusations against Jesus. This was very difficult for them since Jesus obeyed and followed the commandments, one of them being to keep the Sabbath holy. The Pharisees were those who were experts in matters pertaining to Jewish legalism, but had little understanding as to the purpose for the law itself. They seemed to miss the heart of God being blinded by their own bondage to legalism and lack of love.

In response to the accusation made by the Pharisees, Jesus said, "The Sabbath was made for man, and not man for the Sabbath" (Mark 2:27). Jesus was articulating the purpose and spirit of the law. He was telling them, "You have missed the entire purpose for the Sabbath day because you are bound by legalistic opinions and interpretation of God's command. Do you not realize that picking corn for food has absolutely nothing to do with honoring the Sabbath Day? Feeding myself does not violate the Sabbath because it was created so man could be fed and refreshed."

The Pharisees were upset about Jesus being refreshed. They were so concerned about Jesus doing something unlawful on the Sabbath that they failed to keep the commandment of loving their neighbor as themselves. I do not think they would have appreciated being spied on like they were doing to Jesus.

When Jesus spoke to the Pharisees, He addressed their incorrect interpretation of the commandment. They were bound by the "letter of the law" and neglected the spirit and heart of the commandment. This was a common problem with the Pharisees. They were blinded by legalism. They could not see the forest for the trees. Jesus knew the Father's purpose for the commandment of remembering the Sabbath. It had already been articulated clearly in the Word of God.

> Therefore the children of Israel shall keep the Sabbath, to observe the Sabbath throughout their generations as a perpetual covenant. It is a sign between Me and the children of Israel forever; for in six days the LORD made the heavens and the earth, and on the seventh day He rested and was refreshed.
>
> —EXODUS 31:16–17

There are some today who have taken the account of Jesus' confrontation of the Pharisees concerning the Sabbath Day and made a doctrine that it no longer matters if you set aside a day to honor the Lord or not. The argument that is made is Jesus abolished the observance of the Sabbath day by precept, example, and in His sacrificial offering. I assure you my friend, nothing could be further from the truth.

The first thing we must understand is that Jesus did observe the Sabbath. He frequented the Synagogue on a regular, weekly basis. By His example, Jesus upheld the fourth commandment and He kept the Sabbath Day holy unto the Lord. It was a habit He had developed since His birth.

> So He came to Nazareth, where He had been brought up.
> And as His custom was, He went into the synagogue on
> the Sabbath day, and stood up to read.
>
> —LUKE 4:16

The example Jesus left for you and I to follow was to go to church on a weekly basis. He exampled honoring the Lord on the Sabbath day. Everything that Jesus taught and demonstrated upheld the principle and commandment of keeping the Sabbath Day holy unto the Lord. If Jesus had wanted to abolish this commandment then He would have said so in an unambiguous fashion. He had an opportunity to do so when He responded to the accusation of the Pharisees against Him, but did not do so. He only restated the commandment with a clearer understanding of God's divine purpose. That certainly does not classify as an abolishing of this important commandment.

Jesus went to church on a weekly basis. We do not have his attendance records with us today, but we do have the words of the Bible that declare it was His custom to go to the synagogue on the Sabbath day. Jesus was a faithful member of His local church. If we are to follow the example of Jesus, then we will go to church on a regular weekly basis.

117

Jesus had an understanding of Levitical Law, but His obedience was not born out of mere adherence to a code of conduct. He had an understanding of the heart of the Father as to why the commandment was there in the first place. Jesus never said he abhorred the commandments in their purest form. Rather, He confronted the religious traditions of men that discredited and dishonored the commandments that the Father had given to men.

When Jesus laid down His life to pay the price for our redemption and make a way for God's grace to be extended to all of mankind, there is no scriptural indication that the Ten Commandments were abolished. There were some things that were done away with, but the Ten Commandments were not. Hence, the commandment of keeping the Sabbath Day holy remained relevant for those in the New Covenant.

There has been great controversy over the Ten Commandments in days past. In a recent incident, a monument of the Ten Commandments was removed from a public building. Christians were appalled and angry, and I was one of them. It was unthinkable that in the United States of America, a nation that was founded on biblical principles, that something of this magnitude could happen. As I was watching some of the news coverage of this on television, the thought came to me that many Christians took greater offense over the monument being removed than those who do not adhere to the Commandments. I am not saying that we should not be outraged because I myself was. However, if we are going to be infuriated about the removal of a monument of the Ten Commandments, we should certainly be following and obeying them or else we are nothing more than what Jesus described as a hypocrite.

Again, it deserves to be repeated that the Sabbath Day originated at the time of creation, not the Law. It is a divine principle that the Father initiated in the beginnings of time, as we know it. It is more than a commandment, law, or regulation; it is a statute that was instituted the day following the creation of man.

In the writings of the apostle Paul, he restates many of the Ten Commandments. Paul would not reaffirm any of these if they were not relevant for believers in the New Testament. Not only did Paul articulate these commandments, but he also practiced all of them including keeping the Sabbath Day holy.

> And he reasoned in the synagogue every Sabbath.
>
> —ACTS 18:4

Notice it did not say some Sabbaths, but *every* Sabbath. Paul was committed to obeying the Ten Commandments. Paul was committed to honoring the Lord by honoring the Sabbath Day. He knew the Sabbath was intended for the convocation of believers so he went to church.

We may think we have some challenges getting to house of the Lord on Sunday mornings, but I assure you that very few have ever had the challenges that the apostle Paul was presented. To go and preach in the synagogues meant he would have to put his life on the line. His reputation was not good in the Jewish community. He was not a "sought after" speaker for the Jewish synagogue circuit. However, his commitment to obey God was greater than his love for his own life. He had come to the place where he loved not his own life unto the death. (See Revelation 12:11.)

It amazes me today how some believers are so easily removed from a place of obedience by some of the smallest circumstances. If Junior has a hangnail then it is good enough reason for them to not go to the house of the Lord. The last episode of their favorite Sunday sitcom is much more important than a church service. After all, they would "absolutely die" if they missed their favorite television show. What are our priorities? Where is the heart of obedience and commitment?

Some have used the word *grace* to excuse the non-adherence to any commandment that may restrict their behavior. We have heard things such as, "If your conscience does not bother you then it's

OK." While I will concede there are some things God has left for matters of personal conviction, when a conscience is seared any action becomes virtuous. Even the disobedience of clearly articulated commandments is tolerated when your conscience no longer troubles you. Anyone who gets to this place will be led by the enemy into a place of captivity.

Grace does not excuse anyone from obeying the Bible. It is quite the contrary. Grace enables us to obey and fulfill what God has told us to do. Grace gives us the ability to obey from our hearts with the understanding of God's divine purpose. Grace is what has now caused His commandments to be written upon the tablets of our hearts. We are not merely adhering to a code of conduct that has been prescribed and forced upon us. We are the sons and daughters of God who delight in obeying His commands.

Grace is what gives us power to overcome sin and self-will. Grace empowers us to fulfill the call of God upon our lives. Grace is not and never will be an excuse to participate in fleshly and sinful behavior. Neither will it ever legitimize the annulment of God's commandments in the life of believers.

When Jesus died at Calvary, the Bible declares that He removed the handwriting of ordinances that were against us as they were nailed to the cross in Him. (See Colossians 2:14.) The apostle Paul wrote this to the church at Colosse. Some have interpreted this to say that all commandments that were in the Old Testament have been negated and that they are not applicable to those living under the New Covenant. If that were true, Paul was double-minded and double-tongued. It was Paul who also reiterated many of the commandments that were written in the Old Testament. If he meant that all laws and ordinances were abolished, then why did he talk of them in letters that he wrote to different churches?

"Honor your father and mother," which is the first commandment with promise: "that it may be well with you and you may live long on the earth."

—EPHESIANS 6:2–4

These are the writings of Paul where he makes it clear that the commandment of honoring our parents has not been annulled. Paul also talks of how God despises adultery, stealing, murder, lying, and covetousness, which are all forbidden by the Ten Commandments. (See Galatians 5:19–21.) He says those who practice such things will reap the "wrath of God" that is "coming on the sons of disobedience" (Col. 3:6).

Paul in no way insinuated in any of his writings that any of the Ten Commandments had been invalidated. He actually said the complete opposite. He repeatedly verified the importance of the Ten Commandments. Once again, grace never annulled any of the Ten Commandments including the commandment of keeping the Sabbath Day holy.

Any pastor who teaches on the Ten Commandments runs the risk that someone will become an extremist, just as the Pharisees in Jesus' time were. Error always lives next door to truth. Any truth that is taken to an extreme will result in error. Likewise, any person who takes the commandment of keeping the Sabbath Day holy to an extreme position will fall into the ditch of legalism.

There are some basic principles that we must understand in order for there to be proper interpretation of this commandment. First, God created the Sabbath for man to rest and be refreshed both spiritually and naturally. Secondly, the Sabbath is not restricted to a certain day of the week (I will explain more about this later). Thirdly, keeping the Sabbath Day holy is a spiritual issue of the heart—one which God wants to be acted out in the natural. The fourth principle is that doing work on the Sabbath Day is not totally forbidden.

God had the man He had just created in mind when He initiated the setting apart of the Sabbath Day. Perhaps He realized that man would become a workaholic if he were not instructed to take a day of rest. The end result would be premature death for man. There would also be no fruitful relationships outside of business if man were not told to take a day off. God wanted man to take time to smell the roses.

Since God created us, He obviously knows what we need. He knew we would need a day to rest and be refreshed spiritually. He knew that believers would need to assemble themselves together and draw strength from one another. Therefore, God initiated and demonstrated the setting apart of the Sabbath Day in the beginning. It is more than a commandment, it is a principle of the Kingdom of God.

The fact that the Sabbath is not restricted to a certain day of the week may be confusing to some so allow me to explain this in greater detail. The Sabbath Day was the seventh day of the week. It was the day that was to be consecrated to the Lord. In the Jewish culture, that day was used as a time to gather together for the purpose of worship, teaching, and encouraging one another. The day that was set apart for the observance of the Sabbath was Saturday, since it was the last day of the week. However, notice what Paul says to the church at Corinth when addressing them.

> Now concerning the collection for the saints, as I have given orders to the churches of Galatia, so you must do also: On the first day of the week let each one of you lay something aside, storing up as he may prosper, that there be no collections when I come.
>
> —1 CORINTHIANS 16:1–2

It appears from this letter the apostle Paul wrote, that the church at Corinth met together on the first day of the week or Sunday. Sunday was their Sabbath Day. It was the day they had consecrated and set apart for the assembly of the church. Let me share with you some quotes from some recognized theologians concerning this subject and this passage of Scripture.

> It appears from the whole that the first day of the week, which is the *Christian Sabbath*, was the day on which their principal religious meetings were held in Corinth and the churches of Galatia; and, consequently, in all other places where Christianity had prevailed. This is a strong argument for the keeping of the Christian Sabbath.[1]
>
> —ADAM CLARKE'S COMMENTARY

> That there is here clear proof that the first day of the week was observed by the church at Corinth as *Holy Time*. If it was not, there can have been no propriety in selecting that day in preference to any other in which to make the collection. It was the day which was set apart to the duties of religion, and therefore an appropriate day for the exercise of charity and the bestowment of alms. There can have been no reason why this day should have been designated except that it was a day set apart for religion, and therefore deemed a proper day for the exercise of benevolence toward others.[2]
>
> —BARNES' NOTES

> First day of the week-already kept sacred by Christians as the day of the Lord's resurrection, the beginning day both of the physical and of the new spiritual creations; it gradually superseded the Jewish seventh day Sabbath.[3]
>
> —JAMIESON, FAUSSET, AND BROWN COMMENTARY

> The first day of the week, *kata mian sabbaton*, (Luke 24:1), the Lord's day, the Christian holiday, when public assemblies were held and public worship was celebrated, and the Christian institutions and mysteries (as the ancients called them) were attended upon; then let every one lay

by him. It is a day of holy rest; and the more vacation the
mind has from worldly cares and toils the more disposition has it to show mercy: and the other duties of the day
should stir us up to the performance of this; works of
charity should always accompany works of piety.[4]

—MATTHEW HENRY'S
COMMENTARY ON THE WHOLE BIBLE

We can readily see from all of the above commentaries how the
early Church met on Sunday. In becoming the Christian Sabbath
it was indicated that God never meant for the Sabbath Day to be
legalistically observed on Saturday. However, there was to be one
day out of the seven that was to be delegated as a day of Sabbath
observance. Let's look at another Scripture that bears this out.

Now on the first day of the week, when the disciples
came together to break bread, Paul, ready to depart the
next day, spoke to them and continued his message until
midnight.

—ACTS 20:7

Here again we see how the disciples (the Church) assembled
together on the first day of the week. They had a rather lengthy
service with Paul preaching into the wee hours of the next morning. Interestingly enough, the Greek word used for first day of
week is *Sabbaton*. Its origins are in the Hebrew word *Sabbath*. The
first day of the week, Sunday, became the Christian Sabbath.

They came together upon the first day of the week, which
they called the Lord's day (Rev 1:10), the Christian Sabbath, celebrated to the honour of Christ and the Holy
Spirit, in remembrance of the resurrection of Christ, and
the pouring out of the Spirit, both on the first day of the
week. This is here said to be the day when the disciples
came together, that is, when it was their practice to come

together in all the churches. Note, The first day of the week is to be religiously observed by all the disciples of Christ; and it is a sign between Christ and them, for by this it is known that they are his disciples; and it is to be observed in solemn assemblies, which are, as it were, the courts held in the name of our Lord Jesus, and to his honour, by his ministers, the stewards of his courts, to which all that hold from and under him owe suit and service, and at which they are to make their appearance, as tenants at their Lord's courts, and the first day of the week is appointed to be the court-day.[5]

—MATTHEW HENRY'S
COMMENTARY ON THE WHOLE BIBLE

It appears from all that can be gathered that God gave some option as to when the Sabbath would be observed. It was still to be observed, but the day of the week was not written in stone. By all indications, the early Christians observed the Sabbath Day on a different day of the week than the Jewish Sabbath. Those in the early Church observed the Sabbath on Sundays for the most part. This observance has continued even to the present day Christian Church.

I believe there is much conjecture that can be made from these facts. I have always attempted to keep my personal opinion away from doctrinal issues that affect the lives of other believers. Yet on this issue, we must be able to bring an application of Godly wisdom and judgment in order to establish a premise from which we as believers can operate.

One factor in determining our observance of the Sabbath Day is the day of the week that the majority of people do not have any work responsibilities. That is determined by the culture where we live and work. In the areas where most Christians live, Sunday is the day when most people do not have to work.

In the United States, there was a time when hardly anything

125

was open for business on Sunday. Department stores were closed the entire day for observance of the Christian Sabbath. Today, it is much different. There are still many places that do not open on Sundays, but there are many that do. Logically, Sunday is the best day for Christians to observe the Sabbath (day of rest) and gather together. God called for the Sabbath to be a holy convocation. It is difficult for believers to gather together on a day when everybody is working. Sunday, for the vast majority of us, should be our Sabbath since we are not working on that day.

The majority of Christians that do not attend church on Sunday lay out not because of reasons of work or employment. They do so because of laziness and heart issues. They do not keep the Sabbath Day holy because they do not want to. This is offensive to the Lord. If you are this kind of believer, I would encourage you to repent and allow God to revive within you a passion and zeal for His house. It was said of Jesus that "Zeal for Your house has eaten me up" (John 2:17). If that was said of Jesus, let it also be said of us.

People who cannot make the church service for an unavoidable legitimate reason are not going to be the offenders of the commandment. It is the ones who have no desire or determination to be in the house of the Lord or keep the Sabbath Day holy. These are the ones who will insult the Lord with their disobedience. I say none of these things to condemn anyone. However, I do want us to realize exactly what we are doing if we snub the house of the Lord.

I know there are some who are asking the question, "What about people who have jobs that force them to work on Sundays?" This is a very good and legitimate question. I want to answer this question by first articulating something I mentioned earlier. The observance of the Sabbath did not forbid any and all types of work.

Anything you do, whether it is getting up out of bed, there is some kind of work involved. Anytime you expend energy to do anything there is work involved. When you breathe, your lungs are working. When you look at something, your eyes are having to work. By that definition of work, we are always working. Hence, we cannot become legalistic in our view of the Sabbath and miss the heart of God. Again, the purpose of the Sabbath Day was to rest and be refreshed and to conduct an assembly of believers.

The Sabbath did not forbid people from doing basic tasks that were necessary for daily living and survival. It allowed for Jesus to pick corn on the Sabbath (Jesus would not have done it if it did not). It allowed people to lead their ox to water. It gave compensation for emergency situations such as a beast of burden having to be lifted out of the ditch.

There is the principle of interpreting Scripture in light of other Scripture. We have a command in the Bible to respect and honor our employers. (See Colossians 3:22–24.) We are told to be diligent in our work and to have a good attitude at our place of employment. In our application of the principle and command of keeping the Sabbath Day holy, we must balance it with other Scriptures that speak of Christian responsibility to our employers.

There are some places of employment that require their employees to work on Sundays. I do not believe God is upset with someone for having to work on a Sunday. Although, I do not believe it is God's best for that individual to be required to work and not be able to attend church.

This is my counsel to someone who is in that position. First of all, pray for the favor of God. Then go to your employer and let him know of your desire to have Sundays off if possible. Do not become demanding or obnoxious. Make your request known in a way that they can receive it and believe God for a favorable answer. Be willing to make concessions so that you can make three steps towards the five that need to take place. If your employer is unwilling to budge at all, then you may want to consider believing God for a better job.

I recognize that in the United States today there are many people who have to work on Sundays. Most of them do not have to work every Sunday. So, when you are not working, make sure you are in the house of the Lord.

In our church, we have services three times a week. Most of the people who have jobs, where they have to work on Sundays, still make it for at least part of one of our Sunday services. They may have to leave early or arrive late, but they still make every attempt to attend church. God will do things in the lives of these kinds of people. Let this kind of commitment be an example for all of us.

The Sabbath Day is a day that God desires to be set apart for Him. It is a time when we are to come together as the body of Christ to be refreshed spiritually. As we choose to obey this important commandment and hold it in high regard, God will bring forth His blessing within our lives. There are blessings promised to those who will hear and obey the voice of the Lord. Make a choice today to be one of God's obedient, faithful, and committed children.

But you have come to Mount Zion and to the city of the living God, the heavenly Jerusalem, to an innumerable company of angels, to the general assembly and church of the firstborn who are registered in heaven.

—HEBREWS 12:22–23

Chapter 10

WHY MEMBERSHIP?

*I*T IS IMPORTANT for every Christian to be a member of a local church. The local church is the tangible, physical display of the Body of Christ in our local communities. It is the perceptible manifestation of the spiritual house of the Lord on a local corporate level.

From this passage of Scripture, I would like to draw your attention to the words "who are registered in heaven." The word *registered* means to write off, a copy, list, or enrollment. The writer of Hebrews informs us that there are records that are kept in heaven. When someone accepts Jesus as their Savior by confessing Him as Lord of their lives, their name is "registered in heaven" as a member of the Corporate Body of Christ—a member of the Church. There is a list of names of those who are enrolled as members of the Church of the Lord Jesus Christ.

There is identification of those who have been washed in the blood of Jesus.

The moment that someone is born again, they are enrolled in God's Academy of Maturity. The only way to become enrolled in this academy is to join the Church by spiritual regeneration. From that point on, God begins to work with that individual, as a member of the Body of Christ, to bring forth the full character of Christ within their lives.

Heaven is not a place of disorganization. There is great order and proper arrangement of all things including the members of the Church. The records Heaven keeps are very detailed because at a later time, the Judgment Seat of Christ, those who are enrolled will be rewarded according to their achievements and advancements in God's Academy. Heaven is not a slipshod operation. Heaven does not "fly by the seat of its pants." There is great organization and detail given to every thing that transpires and happens in the Church.

We must understand that Heaven is our pattern. Jesus said to pray, "Your kingdom come, Your will be done on earth as it is in heaven." If there is membership in heaven and organization to go along with that membership, then we on earth should mirror the same pattern. If there is enrollment in heaven, then there should be enrollment on earth. In other words, there should be a membership roll for every local church.

> Then I was given a reed like a measuring rod. And the angel stood, saying, "Rise and measure the temple of God, the altar, and those who worship there."
>
> —REVELATION 11:1

Now I realize that some of the book of Revelation is written allegorically, but I also believe there are principles that we can glean. Notice that the heavenly pattern is to measure those who were worshipping in the temple. Obviously, the Lord is not talking about recording each individual's physical measurements. He was not instructing for height and weight of each individual to be taken. The way to measure people is by counting them numerically. To measure the people who were worshipping in the temple, there had to be some form of accounting that recorded who was there.

In chapters two through four of the book of Revelation, there are particular letters that John writes to specific local churches. May I even say that they were written to the pastors of those particular local churches. Let's examine one of them to get an idea of the principle to which I am referring.

> "To the angel of the church of Ephesus write, 'These things says He who holds the seven stars in His right hand, who walks in the midst of the seven golden lampstands: "I know your works, your labor, your patience, and that you cannot bear those who are evil. And you have tested those who say they are apostles and are not, and have found them liars; and you have persevered and have patience, and have labored for My name's sake and have not become weary. Nevertheless I have this against you, that you have left your first love. Remember therefore from where you have fallen; repent and do the first works, or else I will come to you quickly and remove your lampstand from its place—unless you repent. But this you have, that you hate the deeds of the Nicolaitans, which I also hate. He who has an ear, let him hear what the Spirit says to the churches...."
>
> —REVELATION 2:1–7

Notice the letter starts by being addressed to an individual at a particular place, the angel at the (local) church of Ephesus. This letter was not written to just anybody in the body of Christ. There are truths that we can all derive from this letter and it is the Word of God, but it was a *rhema* word for one individual. God told Noah to build a boat and it is recorded in the Bible, but that does not mean we all should become ship manufacturers.

In the body of this letter, the Lord addresses particular things that are going on in that local church. He is not addressing the local church at Sardis at that moment, although he does later.

At the end of the letter he uses the word *churches.* He did not say *church* (singular); he said *churches* (plural). The fact that it is stated *churches* means that God recognizes not just the Universal Body of Christ, which is the Church, but he also recognizes individual local church bodies.

Each one of those individual bodies was made up of members; just like your body has members. The members of your body are not casual attendees. They are connected to you permanently unless you have one of them removed. Likewise, every local church should have members who are accounted for and enrolled.

If you woke up one morning and one of your fingers was missing, you would wonder what had happened. You would begin to try to acquire an answer as to where your finger went. You would do this because your finger is supposed to be connected to your body. I trust that you are beginning to see the picture of why local church membership is biblical and important.

Some have felt that local church membership accounting is not necessary today. They fail to see the importance of being a member of a local church. Many of these same people will quote verses of Scripture from Paul's writings to the Corinthian church stating how we are members of one another in Christ. What they fail to realize is who Paul is addressing. He begins by saying, "To the church of God which is at Corinth" (1 Cor. 1:12; 2 Cor. 1:2). He is addressing a particular local body of believers. These believers were members of the local church located in the city of Corinth.

Local church membership is important and is patterned in the early church. There were official records that were kept. Let's examine how this began in the earliest beginnings of the church.

> And in those days Peter stood up in the midst of the disciples (altogether the number of names was about a hundred and twenty)...
>
> —ACTS 1:15

We see how there was a count made of how many people were present and were part of the disciples. There is an indication that there was some kind of roll that was being kept as it speaks of the "number of names." It did not say the number of individuals or persons, it says the number of names. Names were recorded as to who were a part of the disciples. These are some of the first indications of local church membership that we see.

Be aware that the church at Jerusalem was in its infancy, but being approximately one month old, was already keeping some kind of record of names and attendance. This was obviously of great importance to them seeing how that it is specifically mentioned in the book of Acts. It must have been of great importance to God since He inspired the writer of Acts to pen it. If it was of great importance to the early church and to God, then it should be of great importance to us.

Before we go any further on this subject, I want to state clearly that local church membership does not save you. You are not redeemed because you join a local church and have your name added to a membership roll. There is nothing that will produce the fruit of salvation in your life other than faith in the sacrificial work that Jesus wrought at Calvary. However, this does not mean that it is unimportant for us to be official members of a local church.

> Then Peter said to them, "Repent, and let every one of you be baptized in the name of Jesus Christ for the remission of sins; and you shall receive the gift of the Holy Spirit. For the promise is to you and to your children, and to all who are afar off, as many as the Lord our God will call." And with many other words he testified and

exhorted them, saying, "Be saved from this perverse generation." Then those who gladly received his word were
baptized; and that day about three thousand souls were
added to them.

—ACTS 2:38–41

On the Day of Pentecost, after a tremendous outpouring of the
Holy Spirit, Peter stands and preaches in the streets of Jerusalem.
As a result, there is a multitude who become Christians. At the
end of Peter's invitation, they did not just send everybody home
and say, "Come back and see us." There was a physical count of the
ones who had made a decision to become Christians. To be able to
say that three thousand souls were added means they counted the
recorded names of those who were saved and thus became members. There were three thousand names added to the 120 names
that were already recorded.

One of the key words found in this passage that verifies the
need for local church membership is the word *added*. This means
the people that received salvation were counted and then added to
the ones who were already a part of the church.

There are some today who would try to discredit formal church
membership. The argument is made that it is unnecessary and God is
not concerned about counting or keeping record of who is a part of
the church. They go on to say that God is ultimately keeping records
and the only thing that really matters is that you are saved.

While I will agree that the most important thing in your life is
that you are washed in the blood of Jesus and have experienced spiritual regeneration, this in itself does not mean God is not interested
in formal records being kept of who is joined with the local church
in heart and spirit. Some believers, in their attempt to not be bound
by religious tradition, have fallen into the ditch on the other side of
the road called disorder. Yes, God does keep records and His are the
ones that ultimately matter. However, we are given the responsibility to reflect here on earth what is going on in heaven.

A fact to consider in dealing with this subject is there is an entire book of the Bible called Numbers. This book is involved to a great deal with the numbering, ordering, and organization of God's covenant people. God places importance on divine order.

In the book of Revelation, it speaks of the Book of Life where names are written. These names are those who have been washed in the blood of Jesus. It is needful for us to observe that in heaven there are names and records that are kept. Jesus said that it is these names that are recorded in the Book of Life that He will confess before the Father and the angels in heaven. (See Revelation 3:5.) Once again, we can readily see that God does place some emphasis on names being written down and records being kept.

We see from the previous passage of Scripture in Acts, that three thousand people came to know the Lord in one day and then joined the church at Jerusalem. They immediately began to attend church on a regular basis. They got planted.

> Then those who gladly received his word were baptized; and that day about three thousand souls were added to them. And they continued steadfastly in the apostles' doctrine and fellowship, in the breaking of bread, and in prayers.
>
> —Acts 2:41–42

Notice that after these people were born-again and baptized they "continued steadfastly in the apostles' doctrine." These new converts were hearing the apostles preach and teach on a regular basis. Where were they hearing them? They attended church services so they could learn the truths of the New Covenant. They had to be hearing the apostles on a regular basis in order to continue in their doctrine. You certainly cannot continue in something that you do not know about. These believers immediately became faithful members of the church at Jerusalem.

The New International Version and Revised Standard Version say that "they devoted themselves" to the teachings of the apostles. These believers were fully committed to the local church in Jerusalem. To be devoted means you are faithful, loyal, dedicated, constant, and committed. These new believers understood the importance of being in the house of the Lord and gathering together. They devoted themselves to hearing the Word and fellowshiping together.

You must understand that these things transpired before the day of recorded media and television. In order to have devoted yourself to the doctrine of the apostles, you would have to be with the apostles. You had to gather together to hear the preaching of the Word of God. No one was staying at home and watching Peter's television broadcast. They did not order the cassette copy of the teaching online. Although there is nothing in itself wrong with these forms of communication, they are never to replace the Ekklesia; the assembly of the believers. They were gathering together on a regular basis.

I realize that some folks ask the question, "If I am saved then why do I need to join the church? After all, I am already a part of the family of God and the Bible says I am a fellow member of the Body of Christ." I believe this is a reasonable question that deserves an answer and explanation.

I want to give you seven reasons why you should become a member of a local church.

1. The first reason is your formal membership is a statement of your faith that you are saved and a member of the Body of Christ. I realize that local church membership does not cause anyone to be born again. Neither does water baptism, yet I believe we should still be baptized. Just as water baptism is an outward expression of an inward possession, so formal local church membership is an outward expression and declaration of who you are as a result of spiritual regeneration, a member of the Body of Christ.

I have told the members of our church that becoming a member does not save you for it is required that you be saved before you can become a member. Local church membership does not save you, but saved people should become committed members.

2. The second reason for local church membership is for the purpose of public declaration that you will be planted in that local church. It is important that we make a public declaration that we believe we are where God has called us to be planted. We must make a commitment to the leaders and other members of the local church that we are there to stay. It is easy to be uncommitted when you never make a commitment. Many today are fearful of commitment because they do not like responsibility. If we will make the commitment, God will give us the strength and ability to fulfill that dedication. There will be grace extended for the responsibility.

3. The third reason for local church membership is for personal stability. I have found that those who will formally join a local church and then follow through with their commitment are much more stable than those who do not. Spiritual stability will be the end result of those who will get planted and remain planted. Local church membership is an important ingredient that is necessary in the spiritual planting process. Stability comes as the result of a strong root system. To have spiritual roots that go deep, you must be planted.

4. The fourth reason for local church membership is for corporate local church stability. The leaders of the local

church must have knowledge of whom they can begin to work with and then delegate different responsibilities. A local church cannot thrive in the midst of instability. There must be those who will be consistent in their attendance. A pastor cannot ask at the beginning of every service, "Is there a musician in the house?" He must have musicians he can count on. The congregation must have consistency in the ministry to keep them from feeling "jerked around." A congregation is never more stable than the consistency of its leaders and members in their attendance and ministry.

5. The fifth reason for local church membership is the spiritual benefits that flow out to every area of your life. Those who are members of a local church are more likely to attend (and should do so). There are numerous benefits that have been scientifically proven. Those who attend church on a regular basis have been proven to live on an average of eight years longer than those who do not. Single people who attend church are more than seven times less likely to have premarital sex and cohabit (live together). Being a member of a local church has the potential of touching and affecting every area of your life, if you will be committed to that house of worship.

The testimonies that have been articulated throughout this book belong to those who were members of a local church. They did not merely attend on a regular basis, they had entered into a covenantal relationship with those of like precious faith. Breakthrough was the result of their faithfulness as a member of the local church body. You can have the same testimony too if you will get "plugged in" to the local church where God wants you.

There is a woman in our church who became a member several years ago. When she first began to attend, she was very shy, introverted, and backwards. As a result of becoming a member of the church, God began to revolutionize her life. Here is a portion of her testimony relating to one area of her life that was dramatically affected.

> I appreciate Pastor Stacey when she gets out of her comfort zone. As I see her stretching and going beyond, it encourages me and gives me hope that I can do the same. I also appreciate that she raises the bar when it comes to grooming for women in the Christian community. I was happy to follow her lead. Gradually I started to take time to do my hair and make-up every day even though I am a stay at home mom. I also started dressing nicely like other ladies in the church and *it feels great*! I am more confident than I have ever been. That is priceless! I look at professional women in the marketplace sometimes and think, "You could use a makeover, too!"
>
> My entire self-image has changed as a result of being in the church. I feel like a new person. I no longer am having my "pity parties" and have been set free of feeling like a victim. My life and family have been transformed!

My friend, there are great benefits of being a faithful member of a local church. This young lady could have stayed at home and continued to have her pity party, but instead decided to get planted and allow her life to be changed. You will end up becoming what you are around. She ended up becoming what she saw demonstrated in the church. She saw excellence and an overcoming attitude. She became the same.

6. The sixth reason for local church membership is for fellowship and relationship. One of the reasons that we fellowship is so that we do not become the only fellow in the ship. If we do not relate to those of like precious faith on a regular basis, we will begin to feel

alone, disconnected, and disjointed. These are things
that actually cause some people to attempt suicide.
This is not God's plan. Remember once again, it is
the banana that gets separated from the bunch that
gets peeled and eaten.

In the early Church, we read how they continued in fellowshiping and the breaking of bread. Fellowship was an important part
of the early Church and is still important today. God said in the
beginning that it was not good for man to be alone. God has not
changed His mind since He spoke those words. It is still dangerous
and harmful to be disconnected from the local church where God
has called you to be planted.

People have a choice today when they fall in love. They can get
married and have a stable family, or they can live together outside
of the marriage covenant and sin against God. For Christians the
choice should be easy—get married. Some believers have decided
to just have a casual relationship with those in the church rather
than a covenantal relationship like God has ordained. Figuratively,
you can choose to either "get married" or "live together" with the
other members of the church. For Christians, this also should be
an easy choice. God desires there to be covenantal relationship.

7. The seventh reason for local church membership is
the opportunity of co-laboring with others. Every
person who is born again has a ministry that God has
given to them. This ministry is designed to edify and
bless other members of the church. The local church
gives us the opportunity to work and labor with others in the kingdom of God. Our membership in the
local church brings us into a covenantal relationship
with the other members of that local church body.
That relationship becomes the open door for our
ministry to begin to be manifested.

As iron sharpens iron, So a man sharpens the countenance of his friend.

—Proverbs 27:17

There are great benefits in working and laboring with others. As you begin to endeavor with others in the local church, your gift and ability will be sharpened. It will allow your rough edges to be rubbed off. You will begin to learn from those you are working with in the kingdom of God. The laws of spiritual synergism will begin to work as the combined output of the whole becomes greater than the sum of the individual parts. "One will chase a thousand, and two will put ten-thousand to flight" (Deut. 32:30).

As a pastor, I am not going to allow someone I do not know to get behind the pulpit and preach. I am actually not going to allow them to do much of anything other than worship during the praise and worship portion of the service and sit during the preaching of the Word. Why? It is because I do not know them. The apostle Paul said, "Know those who labor among you" (1 Thess. 5:12). Church membership gives the pastor and the leaders an opportunity to know those who become members better and also lets them (the leaders) know that they (the new members) are committed to the church.

Why should a pastor commit a responsibility to someone he does not know is going to be faithful? This would be very counter-productive. Paul told Timothy to "commit to faithful men who will be able." He did not say "commit to able men and hope they will be faithful." God's first prerequisite for functioning in the church is faithfulness. If you are not faithful, do not get angry with the pastor because he will not allow you to "do your thing." Do not accuse the pastor of squelching your gift and anointing because of your own lack of commitment. He is just obeying the Word of God in not committing any ministry responsibility to you. Show yourself faithful and there will be opportunity.

Before Jesus began His ministry, He was led by the Holy Spirit into the wilderness to be tempted. There His faith was tested and proved. He overcame every kind of temptation. The Bible declares He was tempted in all manners but without sin. (See Hebrews 4:15.) Jesus passed the test and as a result was given a ministry that touched the lives of everyone with whom He came in contact. My friend, if we cannot pass the most basic test of faithfulness as a local church member, how can we ever expect great ministry with effectiveness to be released to us?

For years, I labored faithfully in the church before I ever received a staff position. The pastor did not look at me and say, "Robert, I like you so become a part of our staff." Everyone's work and ministry must be proven. They must successfully walk through the test of faithfulness before great ministry is going to be released to them.

I began my journey in ministry at an early age. I started by using the gifts that God had given to me. I started playing trumpet in the church worship band when I was in eighth grade. Our church had a television program that aired on Sunday mornings. It was broadcast directly from the television station live. My parents would drive me to the studio, and I would play my trumpet.

As my musical ability increased, I began to compose and arrange music for the church band. I got involved in the youth musical ensemble and formed a wind instrument band to play accompaniment.

I continued to be faithful in those areas and as a result was given the responsibility of directing the youth musical group. Today, I have now written hundreds of songs and produced CDs that have been a blessing to many in the Body of Christ. I say none of this for the purpose of fleshly boasting, but only to make the point of the necessity of being a faithful member in a local church.

The road for my journey began when I was young. I did not magically arrive where I am today. Nothing happened because I was more special to God and more favored than others. God will exalt and promote if we will just be faithful members of a local church.

I have had those who would come to my office and tell me of their great plans for future ministry. They would tell me how God had called them to be one of the fivefold ministry gifts in the Body of Christ. As I listened to some of these believers I thought to myself, "You can't even get to church on time the once a month that you attend."

It is amazing that many people feel just because they have been called by God to full-time ministry, it excludes them in some way from basic Christianity 101. You must pass First Grade before you can proceed to High School. I do not want to discourage anyone from pursuing their divine destiny in ministry, but to be successful you will have to master the basics before you get to the advanced. You cannot neglect the basic Christian responsibility of being "plugged in" to a local church. Remember what Jesus said, "Many are called, but few are chosen" (Matt. 22:14). The difference between the called and the chosen is that the chosen are those who show up and are faithful.

It is important for every believer to be a member of a local church. It is a statement of our commitment and consecration to the Lord and that which He has ordained in the earth. As we find the place where God desires for us to be planted, it is important that we begin the planting process by joining that local church. In doing so, we will allow God to begin to work in our lives to bring forth His divine destiny and purpose.

And the LORD God said, "It is not good that man should be alone."

—GENESIS 2:18

Chapter 11

YOU HAVE SOMETHING TO GIVE

*T*HE BIBLE DECLARES that every Christian is a member of the Body of Christ, the Corporate Church of the Lord Jesus Christ. Every member of the body of Christ has something to give. We all have a grace, anointing, or gifting that will be a blessing to others in the local church. None of us are made to be islands to ourselves. God made us to be interdependent.

> The destiny of the Church is my destiny. If you are a member of this One Universal, Many-Membered, Corporate Body of Christ, then your destiny is in the Church, and our destiny is together.
> —DR. BILL HAMON, *THE ETERNAL CHURCH*

After God created Adam and placed him in the garden, He said,

149

"It is not good for man to be alone." What God said to Adam paraphrased is, "Adam, you can't do it by yourself. You need someone to help you." At the beginning of creation, before sin had entered into the environment of perfection, He declares that Adam should not be alone.

If the Almighty and All-Knowing God said in the environment of perfection that Adam was not to be alone (an island to himself), then why do some feel that now, in a less than perfect environment, they can make it without others? The fact is none of us can. None of us are created with that ability. It is not inherent within man to spiritually thrive unconnected from the body of Christ.

The word *alone* is the Hebrew word *bad*. It means "separated" or "a part of the body." God was saying to Adam that it was not good; it was bad, for him to just be a part of the body that is separated from it. There are many members of the body of Christ today who are separated from the body. They are not planted in the house of the Lord.

Any part of my natural body that is separated from the rest of my body will die. It does not have the ability to survive by itself. Every member is dependent on the other. Likewise, without the body of Christ, we will die.

There are many believers today who are spiritually dying and withering away solely because they are not "plugged in" to a local church body. They have become separated from those God called them to be with. We cannot afford for that to happen in our lives. Remember that it is the banana that gets separated from the bunch that gets peeled and eaten.

> But now God has set the members, each one of them, in the body just as He pleased. And if they were all one member, where would the body be? But now indeed there are many members, yet one body. And the eye cannot say to the hand, "I have no need of you"; nor again the head to the feet, "I have no need of you."
>
> —1 CORINTHIANS 12:18–21

Once again, remember that as Paul is speaking in this passage of Scripture, he is talking to a particular local church, that being the church at Corinth. He is emphasizing to them that God has placed the members of that local church there for specific functions and everyone is needed. Not only is every member needed, but each member needs the other members to be able to grow, mature, develop, and succeed.

Your natural body is programmed to function with all of its parts. It cannot function without a heart. It cannot function without lungs. It cannot function without kidneys. Likewise, the local church (body of Christ) needs all of its parts to function in order to thrive.

Our natural bodies can stay alive without some of its body parts. However, it cannot function at full capability. Our bodies can live without our legs, but our mobility will be restricted. Our bodies can live and survive without our hands, but we will be handicapped.

I wonder how many churches today are surviving, yet handicapped, because certain members of that body are not there or functioning. When members of the body are not present or functioning, it causes the body to be incapacitated in certain areas. The solution for this dilemma is for all the members of the body to be planted in the house of the Lord.

The Word of God declares that we are wonderfully made. God has made each of us with a unique gifting and ability. Our own divine ability that God has graced us with is needed by the other members of the church. There is a void in others' lives when we are not there to allow our gift to function and flow.

> From whom the whole body, joined and knit together by what every joint supplies, according to the effective working by which every part does its share, causes growth of the body for the edifying of itself in love.
> —EPHESIANS 4:16

I would like to make several points surrounding this passage of Scripture. The first is that every joint has something to supply. God did not say that some of the joints have something to supply and some have nothing. He said that every member has something to supply the church.

Since we have something to supply, it is important that we supply it. If we do not, the body is lacking in that area. The only way we can supply it is by being with those whom God has called us to be in covenant. That means we must be in the house of the Lord. We must be there to be able to be the supply for others.

I have witnessed through the years how that every member of a local church "brings something to the table." It is amazing how the flow and direction of a service can be altered by certain people being in attendance or not. Their presence to function in their gifting has a profound affect on the service so many times.

One area in which people notice it quickly is that of praise and worship. Any church that has a strong and anointed worship leader has experienced this at some point in time. If there happens to be a service that they are not there, the praise and worship seems to suffer. The absence of their gift in operation changes the flow of the service and sometimes can hinder it. The person that is substituting for them is not an evil individual that seeks to quench the flow of the Holy Spirit. Many times they simply are not gifted in the same manner or have not had time or opportunity to develop their similar gifting to the same degree.

This bears out the importance of everyone functioning in their gifting. You may feel as though your gift is small and insignificant, but I assure you that it is not. Whether you see it or not, when you are not functioning in your gifting, someone else is being affected. It is important for every member of every local church to function.

The next point I would like to make is that every joint of the body is to work. I realize that some people do not like the word *work,* but it is a biblical word. When God put Adam in the garden, he placed him there to work the garden.

> Then the LORD God took the man and put him in the
> Garden of Eden to tend and keep it.
>> —GENESIS 2:15

The word *tend* literally means to work. God expected Adam to work in the garden. His expectation was productivity. God did not want Adam to sit around all day doing nothing. He expected Adam to take care of the garden that He had planted.

Adam was given responsibility. Responsibility involves work. We cannot live a responsible life and not work. Many today feel as though everyone owes them something because they are breathing and alive. My friend, no one owes you a living. To live you must work.

The apostle Paul said if a man does not work, then he should not eat. (See 2 Thessalonians 3:10.) Let me paraphrase this for you. If a man does not work, let him starve. You may say, "Robert, that sounds uncompassionate." Please understand, I did not write the Bible, so you can take it up with the apostle Paul and the Holy Spirit when you get to heaven.

There are believers today who want to complain about not being fed when they are doing nothing in the church. They are not working. They are not putting their hand to the plow. They are spiritually (and many times naturally) lazy. Yet, they feel everyone else in the church owes them something. These Christians attend church and then complain about not being fed spiritually. It is much easier for these people to sit around and criticize others than do something themselves. They are normally the ones who complain the most and contribute the least.

I refer to them as the "spoiled brats" of the Kingdom. They want everything done to their liking and if it is not, they throw a tantrum. Their attitude many times is "my way or the highway."

They leave the church if they are not ministered to in the manner that they have deemed as appropriate for them. May God deliver them from their spiritual "Pampers" and childish ways.

This is a horrible attitude and philosophy of life. It is at the foundation of "welfare mentality." It is at the foundation of false expectations that are never fulfilled. Those who conduct their lives with this attitude become embittered against those who prosper (both spiritually and naturally) and become offended because they themselves are going nowhere.

The Bible clearly articulates that a lazy man will be impoverished. I can pray for God to bring blessing into the life of a lazy man and it will do absolutely nothing until that person gets off their "blessed assurance" and gets a job. They can even sit around, point their finger, and blame everyone else they around, but it will not cause God to sympathize with their position.

Just as it is in the natural, so will it be in the spiritual. Those who do nothing in the church and hide their gift will suffer spiritual lack. They may sit around and point their fingers at others in the church in an attempt to blame them for their own laziness, but it will not "fly" with the Father. We are individually responsible for the work that we are supposed to do.

The spiritual laws that govern the kingdom of God are irrefutable. God instituted them and put them into motion. One of these laws is the law of work. We are commanded to be productive naturally and spiritually. We are commanded to work naturally and spiritually. There is reward for those who abide by this law and consequences for those who do not.

The next point I would like to draw your attention to is that every joint is to do its share. When I was growing up, everyone in our house had certain chores to do. There were responsibilities assigned to each of us. My brother and I did not have to do the same jobs, but we had to do the specific ones that we had been individually assigned.

Likewise, in the house of the Lord, we all have differing responsibilities. We do not all do the same thing. We have different giftings and abilities. I do not have to do what my wife does in the church. I just have to do my assignment. When every member begins to do his or her specific job, the end result is that the church is edified.

I played trumpet in the band when I was in high school. Later on, while a music major in college, I was the principal trumpet in the orchestra. When I played in the band and orchestra, everyone had their own individual part to play. You read from your own individual printed piece of music. I did not play the first clarinet part, nor the second trombone part. I had my own part to play.

The element that made the music beautiful was that everyone played their own part, at the right time in the composition, and played in tune. If everyone had played the same part it would have been musically uninteresting. If those in the orchestra had played their part, but at the wrong time in the composition, it would have sounded chaotic. If everyone had played their part at the right time in the composition, but were out of tune, it would have sounded horrendous.

As it is in the natural, so it is in the spiritual. It is important that we all play our part at the right time and do it with a good attitude. When you do something with a bad attitude it is the same as a musician playing with bad intonation. However, when you play your part correctly, there is beautiful music that is made in the church. People are blessed, edified, and comforted.

We must realize that we are either building up the church by doing our share, or we are tearing down the church by not doing our share. When we do not function in the way we were meant to function, we have an adverse effect on the church. When we do our share, we have a positive effect on the church. What kind of effect do you want to have?

We must all, as members of the body of Christ, put our hand to the plow and begin to work. We all have our share to do. God has given us something that the body needs. We are important members. It behooves us to activate our gifts and abilities so that we may help edify the church.

> As each one has received a gift, minister it to one another, as good stewards of the manifold grace of God.
> —1 PETER 4:10

As you read this passage of Scripture, there are three principles that are evident. The first is that every member of the church has a gift. The second is that we are to minister that gift to others in the church. The third is that we are to be good stewards of His gift that he has bestowed upon us.

It is not possible for us to fulfill any of these commands if we are not actively participating in the house of the Lord. If we are not planted, then how are our gifts going to be revealed, activated, and stirred up? If we are not in the house of the Lord, then how are we going to be trained and who are we going to minister to? If we refuse to obey His command, then how are we going to be classified as good stewards of the grace of God?

We all have something to give. We all have a gift. However, we must be positioned correctly in the church to be able to see that gift mature, develop, and become a blessing to the church. It all starts with being planted in the house of the Lord.

> Now concerning the collection for the saints, as I have given orders to the churches of Galatia, so you must do also: On the first day of the week let each one of you lay something aside, storing up as he may prosper, that there be no collections when I come.
> —1 CORINTHIANS 16:1–2

Another area where we have something to give is finances. God expects us to support the house of the Lord with our tithes (ten percent of our income) and offerings. Tithing is a biblical principle that we find throughout the Word of God. It was practiced before the Law of Moses, during the Old Covenant, and during the early New Testament church. Tithing did not "pass away" with the introduction of grace.

As you see in the above passage of Scripture, Paul had commanded them that when they came together (the first day of the week) they were to receive an offering. The principle stated by Paul was that they were to come together and give financially. They were commanded to give proportionally to how God had blessed them. They did not all have to give the same amount. They were to all give according to how they were being prospered.

Interesting enough, Paul said "on the first day of the week let each of you lay . . . " The word *lay* is the Greek word *tithemi*. The word means "to give." Paul clearly articulated to the church to give their tithe on the first day of the week. I tell our congregation that on the first day of the week tithe-mi or me tithe.

Paul prefaced this by saying, "as I have given orders to the churches in Galatia." There was an order to be followed in the giving and receiving of tithes and offerings. Paul expressed this order when he wrote to the church at Galatia.

> Let him who is taught the word share in all good things with him who teaches. Do not be deceived, God is not mocked; for whatever a man sows, that he will also reap. For he who sows to his flesh will of the flesh reap corruption, but he who sows to the Spirit will of the Spirit reap everlasting life. And let us not grow weary while doing good, for in due season we shall reap if we do not lose heart.
>
> —GALATIANS 6:6–9

The order that Paul gave to the church at Galatia was that those being taught were to give to those who were teaching. The pastoral ministry in the church was to be supported by the weekly tithes and offerings that were being given and received. We see that Paul even begins to share on the relationship of giving and the law of sowing and reaping. He declares that God will cause a financial harvest to come into the lives of those who will be faithful to give.

We have had those who have come into our church with varying degrees of financial needs. I have watched these same people as they received revelation of the principles of giving be transformed financially. I have seen them come from poverty to prosperity.

They started out giving little because they had very little to give. Yet as they were faithful with what they had, God gave them more. As they were faithful with more, then God gave them even more than before. We must understand that God is not mocked and whatever we sow we will reap. It is His principle that He initiated.

If we were able to reap without giving it would be a mockery to God. It would mock Him because it would violate the principle that He put into motion. It would also be a mockery to Him if we sowed and did not reap. I assure you that God will not allow that to happen either.

Here is a wonderful testimony that I believe will encourage you:

> I have been a *tither* for the majority of my Christian life. I have also been a sporadic giver. I believed that obedience to the tithe would meet my needs and that special giving would meet special needs. However, it was being planted in a local body that brought a greater knowledge and understanding for the necessity of continuous giving.
>
> Well into my adult Christian life, my family was led to make a geographic move. Of course in doing that, we also made a church move. The Lord took us to a local body where we became planted. The pastor had a unique slant on giving which he demonstrated at every service. We

would receive the tithes at the beginning of the service and then end every service with an offering. The pastor would say, "Everyone get an offering." I believed in giving free will offerings not required offerings, so I was a reluctant follower.

As the pastor continued to exhort the congregation concerning giving, I was getting angrier at every service. I participated reluctantly. I was obedient, but not willing. I was getting so annoyed and so uncomfortable that I started thinking about leaving the church. When I prayed about leaving, I was convinced that the Lord had planted us there. I also was convinced that you should trust and obey your pastor. I decided to stay where I was planted.

After I committed to willingly obey, the Lord gave me understanding about the principle of continuous giving. I found that through being planted in a local church, my vision and understanding of giving to the Lord was stretched.

As I became willing and obedient, God began to bless us financially. I found that my income almost doubled in one year as I expanded my giving. I found that you did not have to give a lot, but the key was to give consistently.

God has given us all something to give. We have our gifts and abilities. We also have our finances. Jesus said, "Give and it shall be given unto you" (Luke 6:38). He went on to say, "With the same measure you give it will be measured back to you again."

God desires to bring us into a place of abundant provision both spiritually and naturally. What do you want? How much do you want? We can determine our own outcome by our giving.

We all have something to give. As we are faithful with what we have, God will give us more. Let us not deprive the body of Christ by withholding what God has placed within our lives.

His lord said to him, "Well done, good and faithful servant; you were faithful over a few things, I will make you ruler over many things. Enter into the joy of your lord.

—MATTHEW 25:21

Chapter 12

THE FAITHFUL SERVANT

*P*ART OF BEING planted involves being faithful. To be faithful we must be submitted and committed. We are only planted to the degree of our faithfulness and commitment. If our faithfulness and commitment are shallow, then we will be planted shallow and our roots will not go down deep in the soil.

The problem with shallow planting is that the growth and strength of a plant is limited. The growth will be minimal and the strength will be little. A plant that has a shallow root system may be able to survive a small rainstorm, but not the major storms. In a major storm there is a great possibility of that plant being washed away. It is the root system that gives a plant strength and stability.

Your effectiveness in life and ministry is determined by your faithfulness and commitment to the place that God has planted you. If we are once a month attendees, we will not be spiritually strong. If we are not committed to the house of the Lord, we will be unstable. There will be little fruit and effectiveness within our lives spiritually.

As a pastor, I have seen this proven over and over again. We have a counseling ministry in our church called "Restoring the Foundations." It is a six week process that an individual or couples go through. They receive approximately two hours of counseling one night each week. In order to go through this, people have to make a commitment to make their appointments and be at all church services (three a week). The ones who follow through with their commitment come out on the other side changed and revolutionized. The ones who do not follow through with their commitment receive very little, if anything. At the end of the six weeks the unfaithful are virtually unchanged.

Being faithful to the house of the Lord produces great benefit in the life of the believer. Let's examine a parable that Jesus gave concerning faithfulness.

> For the kingdom of heaven is like a man traveling to a far country, who called his own servants and delivered his goods to them. And to one he gave five talents, to another two, and to another one, to each according to his own ability; and immediately he went on a journey. Then he who had received the five talents went and traded with them, and made another five talents. And likewise he who had received two gained two more also. But he who had received one went and dug in the ground, and hid his lord's money. After a long time the lord of those servants came and settled accounts with them. So he who had received five talents came and brought five other talents, saying, 'Lord, you delivered to me five talents; look, I have gained five more talents besides them.' His lord said to him, 'Well done, good and faithful servant; you were faithful over a few things, I will make you ruler over many things. Enter into the joy of your lord.' "He also who had received two tal-

ents came and said, 'Lord, you delivered to me two talents; look, I have gained two more talents besides them.' His lord said to him, 'Well done, good and faithful servant; you have been faithful over a few things, I will make you ruler over many things. Enter into the joy of your lord.' Then he who had received the one talent came and said, 'Lord, I knew you to be a hard man, reaping where you have not sown, and gathering where you have not scattered seed. And I was afraid, and went and hid your talent in the ground. Look, there you have what is yours.' But his lord answered and said to him, 'You wicked and lazy servant, you knew that I reap where I have not sown, and gather where I have not scattered seed. So you ought to have deposited my money with the bankers, and at my coming I would have received back my own with interest. Therefore take the talent from him, and give it to him who has ten talents. For to everyone who has, more will be given, and he will have abundance; but from him who does not have, even what he has will be taken away. And cast the unprofitable servant into the outer darkness. There will be weeping and gnashing of teeth."

—MATTHEW 25:14–30

We can see from this passage of Scripture the importance Jesus places on being a faithful servant. The lord of the house gave each servant talents in differing amounts. They were expected to do something with them. They were expected to produce.

On his return, the lord of the house was furious with the servant who had done nothing. He was so furious that he called him wicked and lazy. He ultimately gave an order to throw the unprofitable servant out of the house and into the darkness.

The wonderful thing in this parable is the end result of the faithful servants. The lord said to them, "I'm going to give you more since you were faithful with what I gave you." The promise is that God will bless the faithful man. He will have more than what he started with. God will activate His multiplication principle in the faithful man's life.

He also says, "Enter into the joy of your lord." The faithful man will be shown favor. The faithful man will have great joy. There is great reward that comes to the faithful.

Every believer has at least one talent or gift that God has given them. They possess the seed of that gift in their lives that will produce a great harvest when planted. God is expecting fruitfulness because he gave us a gift. He did not give us a gift so we could protect it. He gave us a gift because he wants us to use it to bless others. We can either use it or lose it.

The talents and gifts that God has given to us are meant to benefit and bless others. If we do not use what God has given us, the rest of the Church is deprived. Ultimately, God is displeased. If we are going to please the heart of the Father, we must be faithful servants and use what God has gifted us with.

> Having then gifts differing according to the grace that is given to us, let us use them.
>
> —ROMANS 12:6

We see once again the importance of using our gift. Paul commands the Church to *use* what they have been *given*. If we do not use it, God will give it to someone else. If we do not fulfill the call of God, He will raise up someone else that will.

We see this principle with the children of Israel. The generation that came out of Egypt was called to go into the Promised Land. Only two men from that entire generation entered in. God had to raise up their children in their place because of doubt, unbelief, murmuring, and complaining. They would not arise to the challenge, so God raised up an entirely different generation to fulfill His will.

Everyone in the body of Christ is important, but none of us are irreplaceable. If we do not obey, God will find someone who will. If we are not faithful to be planted and do what God has said, then

He will find someone who will be. I do not want to be replaced. Do you?

I have had people come to me and say, "Pastor, I want to be used by God." My response to them is, "Well then, use your gift." The only way to be used by God is to use your gift. Gifts are given and not on loan. You are responsible for using what God has given to you.

Every believer in the body of Christ has a unique gifting and ability. That gifting has been divinely placed within our lives. That gifting is to be a blessing to the church. If we are not planted in the church, we cannot use our gift nor can we be a blessing to the body.

> As each one has received a gift, minister it to one another, as good stewards of the manifold grace of God.
>
> —1 PETER 4:10

To minister one to another we must be planted in a local church. The divine enablements that God releases in our lives are meant primarily to edify and build up the church. If you are not in the house of the Lord, you will not be able to edify the church. That means we must be planted.

Let me give you some food for thought. If we are to be good stewards, is it possible to be bad stewards? What is a bad steward? A bad steward would be one that acts irresponsibly. A bad steward would be one who did nothing with their gift.

Being a good steward starts with using our gift and divine ability. The way that God has designed for that to function and flow begins in the house of the Lord. It is there, the house of the Lord, that your gift will develop. It is there you will be trained and nurtured. It is there you will become acquainted with the people to whom God has called you to minister.

To be a faithful and good steward we must have a servant's heart. Servanthood involves giving of yourself. It involves commitment to God's purpose and will. It may involve some sacrifice at times.

Commitment is a word that we hear less of today. It has almost been lost in the vocabulary of Christians. It seems as though when a leader in the church begins to require a commitment, the accusation is made that they are being "controlling." Call it what you want, but commitment is necessary to be a good steward and a faithful servant.

To be committed means that you will do what you said you would do. Jesus was committed. I am so glad he did not wake up on the day of His betrayal and tell the Father, "I'm too tired today; get someone to fill in for me." Jesus knew His purpose and was committed to the cause.

It is amazing how there are believers who can make a commitment to do something in the church and then at the last minute call and say, "I can't come because I'm tired." I have told them before, "Welcome to Earth." Try calling your employer and telling him you are not coming to work because you are too tired. He will probably follow up with a word to rhyme with tired like "fired." A good steward will follow through with his commitment. A faithful servant will do whatever it takes to get the job done. The faithful man is not a man of excuses.

A good steward is one who has a heart to serve. He does not have to be made to do so. Paul said that God loves a cheerful giver. God loves someone who is prompt to do what needs to be done. Faithful men are those who will go the extra mile and give of themselves so that their commitment is carried out. They will give of themselves whether they feel like it or not.

> For you, brethren, have been called to liberty; only do not use liberty as an opportunity for the flesh, but through love serve one another.
>
> —GALATIANS 5:13

Paul says that we have been called to walk in freedom. I know that we are all thankful for the freedom we have. Yet, please understand that the freedom Paul is referring to does not free us from God-given responsibility and stewardship. Freedom has never negated responsibility. Personal responsibility actually increases because of freedom.

When I was a child, my responsibilities were very small compared to what they are now. When I was a small boy, my mother did the laundry. My father mowed the grass. My parents did the cooking. All my needs were provided by my parents.

The only thing I had to do was eat, sleep, keep my room clean, and do my homework. The flip side of this was that I had little freedom. My parents told me when to wake up, where to go, when I would eat, and when I was to go to bed.

Now I am an adult. I am the father of three wonderful children. I have a lot of freedom. I can go where I want to go. I can eat when I want to eat. I can go to bed when I want to go to bed. The flip side is that I have much more responsibility. I have the responsibility of doing everything for my children that was done for me when I was a child. I trust you get the picture. If you are a parent, you know exactly what I am talking about.

Freedom does not excuse anyone from biblical responsibility. Freedom does not mean you come to church whenever you feel like it and stay home when you do not. Liberty does not mean that you are free to do whatever you want to do whenever you want to do it. There are stewardship issues that must be factored into the equation.

Paul was saying to the church at Galatia, "Do not use your freedom as an opportunity and excuse for your unwillingness to serve" (Gal. 5:13). That's the reason he then says, "But by love serve one another." We cannot use freedom as an excuse for spiritual laziness. Laziness is not freedom, it is bondage. Laziness is sin and missing the mark. Laziness will cause our destiny to go unfulfilled.

God will give you strength if you need it. If you are tired and weary, as you wait on the Lord (serve Him), He will renew your strength. Make the step in the right direction and God will uphold you by His power. If we will follow through as good stewards and faithful servants, God will bless us abundantly in all that we do.

A faithful servant will give of himself without expectation of financial remuneration. Every member in the church cannot be remunerated financially for everything in which they participate. It is a virtual impossibility. There is also no scriptural precedent for it. Throughout Bible history, great men and women of God freely gave of themselves. God, who sees in secret, will reward us openly, if we will have a faithful heart. (See Matthew 6:4.)

The end result of faithfulness is exaltation. God always rewards and exalts those who are faithful to Him. He openly rewards those who will give of themselves cheerfully and hilariously.

As a pastor and an employer, there is nothing any more disappointing than having to continually tell an employee to do their job. If an employer has to tell an employee something twice, they have had to say it one time too many.

The next most disappointing thing is to have an employee do their job with a bad attitude. No employer or pastor enjoys seeing a bad attitude in one of their paid or volunteer workers. If they see it, they will try to bring correction. If it continues, they will find someone else to do the job. I would think that God does something very similar. If we present a bad attitude, He corrects us. If that attitude continues, He replaces us.

In the parable of the talents, the lord referred to the unproductive servant as wicked. The word *wicked* means "hurtful or evil in effect or influence." Jesus said that the servant who did nothing with his gift was a wicked man. Jesus referred him to as one who would hurt the church and be a bad influence.

Laziness is a contagious disease. The writer of Proverbs had a lot to say about the lazy man. None of it was good. The lazy man can be converted, but only if he is willing to work.

We should all be willing to work. We should strive to be good stewards of the gift that God has blessed us with. We should strive to be faithful servants that are productive in the kingdom of God.

There is a family that has been a part of our church for approximately seven years. When they first began to attend, they were looking for a place that they could make as their church home. They had been sporadically attending other churches, but never were really committed to any.

As they began to attend the services and hear the Word of the Lord ministered, they got planted. They became faithful members that gave and labored in the church.

When they first began to come, they had some major problems in their home. Their marriage was in trouble, they were in a lot of debt, their son was performing poorly in school, and the foundations of their lives were very weak. They needed to be restored (understand that restoration is a process, not an overnight miracle).

Together, they began to work faithfully in the church. They would do things for my wife and I without being asked or coached. They would get my briefcase, carry my Bible, pull my car around to the front of the church after the service, and provide pre-service snacks for us in my office. I never asked them to do any of this. They took it upon themselves.

At first, I was very uncomfortable with them doing such things. I considered asking them to stop because I did not want the other members in the church to think I had some kind of indentured servant or that I had requested this from them. As I was considering this, the Lord rebuked me and spoke to my heart, "They need to do this." It was not so much that I needed them to do this, but they needed to serve to activate the blessings of the faithful servant.

As they continued, God began to bring breakthrough in their lives. Their marriage was restored and strengthened. His business began to take off as his personal sales increased dramatically. They were able to eliminate long-standing debt. Their son, who had been on mind altering prescription medication, discontinued usage and began to excel in his school work. They had wanted to adopt a little girl to whom they had been foster parents. My wife and I were able to go to the official signing of adoption documents that granted their desire.

Today they live in a new house, which God blessed them with along with their son and newly adopted daughter. They are doing well financially and are an active part of the leadership team in our church. They also function on one of our post-service ministry teams.

These people were just ordinary people who made a decision to serve someone other than themselves. They ministered to Stacey and I with great diligence. They were faithful in their attendance, their giving, and their serving.

It all begins with being planted in the house of the Lord. We must renew our commitment to serve the Lord by being involved in His house.

> "Is it time for you yourselves to dwell in your paneled houses, and this temple to lie in ruins?" Now therefore, thus says the LORD of hosts: "Consider your ways! You have sown much, and bring in little; you eat, but do not have enough; you drink, but you are not filled with drink; you clothe yourselves, but no one is warm; and he who earns wages, earns wages to put into a bag with holes.".... "You looked for much, but indeed it came to little; and when you brought it home, I blew it away. Why?" says the LORD of hosts. "Because of My house that is in ruins, while every one of you runs to his own house."
>
> —HAGGAI 1:4–6, 9

God puts great emphasis on us prioritizing His house. He puts great emphasis on us using our gifts to edify the church. God wants His house to be strong. The way that He has ordained this to come about is through every member of the church functioning in his or her gift and divine ability and serving each other.

We must make a decision and a commitment that we will allow God to use us by using our gift. We must choose today to be faithful servants and good stewards of the grace of God.

And then many will be offended, will betray one another,
and will hate one another.

—MATTHEW 24:10

Chapter 13

THE ENEMY CALLED OFFENSE

HE NUMBER ONE enemy of believers being planted and staying planted is offense. Offense causes people to erect a fence. We choose to close ourselves off from others when offense comes into our lives. Offense will cause born again Christians to separate from the body of Christ. It will cause those who have a valid ministry in the church to conceal their ministry and defraud the body of Christ.

> Then His disciples came and said to Him, "Do You know that the Pharisees were offended when they heard this saying?" But He answered and said, "Every plant which My heavenly Father has not planted will be uprooted."
> —MATTHEW 15:12–13

As Jesus begins to respond to the question of His disciples, He brings a connection between offense and being planted. Jesus says that those who take an offense will end up being uprooted. It is offense that causes people to leave the church. It is offense that causes believers to break covenantal relationships.

Offense is the one single thing that negatively effects God-ordained relationships more than anything else. It is offense that causes marriages to end in divorce. We must begin to see offense like cancer. It is a cancer that will destroy and must be eradicated from our lives.

I have been guilty of taking an offense before. There are probably very few people, if any, who have never taken an offense because of something that someone else said or did. We must understand the dangers of offense, for it is a destructive force. Offense will cause divine connections in our lives to be severed.

The enemy desires to take any area of our lives where we feel we are being mistreated and turn it into an offense. It is amazing how the enemy can magnify things in our lives as he attempts to destroy relationships. The least things become giant mountains. We must realize the enemy is giving us a false vision so we will be offended and separate ourselves from the body in which we are to belong.

My eye does not belong on another human body. It is made with my DNA. It fits me perfectly. It allows me to be able to see. My eye cannot get offended at my head and decide that it is going to attach itself to another person. Are not you glad that the members of your body are not like the members of the body of Christ?

If the members of our body were like the members of the body of Christ, you would have body parts from people everywhere. Other people would have some of your body parts. I realize this analogy might be a little unorthodox, but we must understand that offense causes believers to do strange things.

An elder in our church had been hired as a staff member. He

loved the Lord, the church, and his job. He seemed to do well for a little while, but I started noticing that he and his personality type were not suitable for the job that we had hired him to do. He had been hired to do a very task oriented job while he was a very people oriented person. He was working diligently and doing his best, but he and the job were not coinciding. After a short time, He was frustrated and I was frustrated with him. We eventually released him from his employment at the church.

Whenever we released him, he was devastated. He had to wrestle with a range of emotions from anger to failure to hopelessness. I could fully understand. Even though we sat and talked about this and were very conscientious in the way it was handled, it still wounded him. There are very few people who can have a good opinion about a boss that terminates their employment. What was worse for him and his wife was that I, his former boss, was also their pastor. You can see the internal conflict that would emerge in this kind of scenario.

He considered leaving the church and I would have understood if he did. As they traveled this emotional roller coaster, they decided to remain planted and not be offended. It was not easy, but they did it successfully.

Today, they are involved in the church to a greater degree than ever before. God has blessed them with fruitful ministry, not to mention all the physical and financial blessings that have transpired. They oversee several major areas of ministry within our church today. I am glad they did not allow an offense to take them from where God had planted them. They were tempted, yet remained true to the call of God upon their lives.

Offense causes believers to detach themselves from the body in which God has called them to be connected. Many times these people become disenchanted with "church" in general. From that point in time they stay home. Just as a member of our physical body will die if it is detached from the rest of our body, they end up spiritually dying. Just as a plant that is uprooted will wither and dry up, the same happens to them.

The word *offense* is the Greek word *skandalon*. It means "a trap or snare." In other words, offense is the bait that the enemy uses to entrap and snare you. John Bevere has a wonderful book out on this entire subject that covers it with great detail. It is entitled *The Bait of Satan*. His book is an exhaustive study on how offense prohibits believers from fulfilling God's plan for their lives. It also brings solutions to this issue that so many believers are ensnared with today.

Offense is the culprit. It is the enemy of the body. It is the spiritual infirmity that has caused many powerful ministries to become non-effective. It has caused members in the body of Christ to become islands unto themselves resulting in spiritual paralysis.

My friend, it is not worth it. Our personal feelings are not to be exchanged for the destruction of God-ordained relationships. We should not allow the divine connections in our lives to be destroyed because our feelings were hurt. God will heal our feelings. If we were wronged, God will make it right. If we were defrauded, God will repay. The relationships that God brings into our lives are much more important than our personal fleshly feelings.

To actually take an offense, we are admitting to selfishness. We are saying that our own feelings and emotions are more important than God's will and purpose for our lives. I realize that this may be a hard pill to swallow, but we need to analyze what we are actually doing when we take an offense. We are saying, "I am the one that is more important. I am more important than our relationship or the will of God."

Understand this is not meant to condemn. If this were meant to condemn, I would be condemning myself. I will be the first one to admit guilt. I feel like the apostle Paul who said, "I am chief" (1 Tim. 1:15) when speaking of sinners. I have personally missed it in this area before.

The good news is that God's grace and mercy is greater than our sin. God will pick us up and restore us if we will let go of our offense. If we will ask Him to forgive us, He will be faithful and just and will cleanse us from all unrighteousness. God will heal and deliver us if we will begin to cry out to Him.

Harboring offense in our lives will produce bitterness. Bitterness will destroy you. Bitterness will cause sickness and disease to be manifested in your body. Bitterness is a destructive force that carries with it substantial consequences. We must release any offense to disable bitterness from taking root in our lives.

> Pursue peace with all people, and holiness, without which no one will see the LORD: looking diligently lest anyone fall short of the grace of God; lest any root of bitterness springing up cause trouble, and by this many become defiled.
>
> —HEBREWS 12:14–15

We see in this passage of Scripture the result of harboring an offense. Bitterness causes others to be defiled. Offense not only negatively affects the one holding the offense, but it also affects others who are around. Bitterness causes trouble in the church.

When someone is offended, they become introverted. As they meditate on the offense, it turns to bitterness. When others in the church notice that they are separating themselves from the body, they ask them, "Are you all right, is everything OK?" The next thing you know, they are voicing their offense with bitterness spewing out to all those around.

If it stopped there it would not be as destructive. Unfortunately, it does not. Some of those who hear this inglorious articulation of offense, take up the offense they have just heard. They are the "defenders." They feel a responsibility to come to the defense of the offended person. The end result is one person's offense is multiplied in the church. It becomes a spiritual cancer in the body.

We cannot afford to take others' offense. We have enough to deal with without taking another's problem. Remember, we are only hearing one perspective and there are two sides to every story. We cannot allow the enemy to use another's offense and bitterness to get us uprooted from the place that God has called us to be planted. We must recognize and discern the plot of the enemy.

> "Not what goes into the mouth defiles a man; but what comes out of the mouth, this defiles a man." Then His disciples came and said to Him, "Do You know that the Pharisees were offended when they heard this saying?"
> —MATTHEW 15:11–12

People become offended for various reasons. One that we specifically see mentioned in the Bible is the preaching of the Word. Jesus was constantly offending the Pharisees and the teachers of the law with His teaching. They despised Jesus. They tried to throw him off a cliff at one point in time. (See Luke 4:29.) This was all because He taught the truth and reality of the kingdom of God.

It is amazing how many times believers will get excited when the Scripture is quoted, "You will know the truth and the truth will make you free" (John 8:32). You can sing songs about the truth and people will rejoice and shout. It seems as though some of the rejoicing stops when the truth shows up. The same ones who were saying "amen" when the Scripture was being quoted are now not so excited with the confrontation of truth.

Jesus was and is the truth. He confronted the religious traditions of man that made God's Word nonproductive. He confronted false teaching. He confronted those who compromised the reality of the kingdom of God. He was hated for it. Those who prided themselves in the law (the Word) hated Him the most.

Many times, when believers in the church are confronted with truth, they become offended. When something is said that cuts across their "old wineskin" or indoctrination, they are upset. When their sacred cow is roasted and barbecued, they do not want to eat the meat. They prefer the milk.

I have seen people leave the church because they were offended over what was being taught. Even though it was scriptural teaching, it was not what they wanted to hear. Paul referred to this as those who have "itching ears" (2 Tim. 4:3). They want their pet doctrine scratched and it is not happening. As a result, they get angry, make accusations, and leave the church. They have to save face; therefore, they find some kind of spiritual justification for their departure.

I understand there will always be differing opinions as it relates to doctrinal issues. Everyone will possess their own personal convictions about varying issues. Although, it is unfortunate when those who are there to be taught become the "expert theologians" who believe they have greater exegetical skill than the pastor. They proceed to communicate with the pastor of the church how that he is mistaken in his interpretation of the Scripture because it does not align itself with their conviction and understanding. When the pastor does not change as a result of their magnificent exposition of theological truth, they are offended, get angry, and leave with a so-called spiritual justification. They "shake the dust off their feet" because their ministry has been rejected. This kind of behavior is ungodly and devilish.

The pastor could possibly be wrong and you might be hurt that he did not receive your counsel, but this is never a reason to leave. It is nothing more than a fleshly excuse. There may be a time that God releases you from that church, but it should not be over issues such as this. It seems as though when someone is looking for an excuse to leave they will surely find one. If they cannot find one, the enemy is usually nearby to provide them with one.

The one you hear the most is, "God told me to leave." Most of these individuals are spiritually hard of hearing and can only hear one thing, "Leave." Actually, their offense is speaking to them. The

Bible says that even the enemy comes as an angel of light, a messenger of revelation. (See 2 Corinthians 11:14.)

God is not saying "leave" in the vast majority of these cases. He actually wants them to deal with their "stuff." The enemy wants them to get out of the place where God has planted them. The enemy wants them to be uprooted and get out of God's will.

Jesus spoke of this in the parable of the sower. He described these as stony ground.

> And these are they likewise which are sown on stony ground; who, when they have heard the word, immediately receive it with gladness; and have no root in themselves, and so endure but for a time: afterward, when affliction or persecution ariseth for the word's sake, immediately they are offended.
>
> —MARK 4:16–17

Believers who are offended easily are those who have no root (they are not planted). It becomes a vicious circle of life for them. They are offended because they have no root. They have no root because they are offended. They become like hamsters on the hamster wheel that are always running, but going nowhere.

Part of the reason for this is that their offense justifies their behavior of not being planted. "The reason I don't go to church is because people are spiteful towards me." This type of justification does not hold up under biblical scrutiny. It is fleshly and devilish.

This is not the plan of God. God desires for us to be planted and not allow any offense to get us out of the garden in which He has planted us. It is in that garden (the local church) where He has planted us that we will grow, mature, and bloom. If we become uprooted because of offense, we will not grow to full maturity and will become unfruitful. We may have some success in the natural, but this does not mean we are succeeding in the kingdom of God.

At the root of offense is unforgiveness. It is a sin that you can only be forgiven of by forgiving the one you are being unforgiving towards. You sow forgiveness and then reap forgiveness. Jesus said that God would not forgive us if we did not forgive others (Mark 11:26).

Unforgiveness will cause your prayers to go unanswered. It blocks up the flow of God's blessings in your life. It will cause your leaves to begin to wilt. Your fruit will begin to taste sour. We must learn to forgive quickly to keep the flow of God's blessings and fruitfulness in our lives.

One of the reasons that believers become offended is disagreement. It is all right to disagree but not be disagreeable. People who have an argumentative spirit end up becoming spiritual brawlers in the church. They become weeds in the garden that choke out the life of the good plants. They can be converted to a good plant if they will allow the Lord to deliver them from that weed seed attitude.

Being argumentative and disagreeable is never edifying. It is destructive behavior. Jesus said to "agree with your adversary quickly" (Matt. 5:25). If we are to agree with our adversary, then how much more should we operate our lives with a spirit of cooperation and agreeability in the church?

We will never agree with everyone one hundred percent of the time. I love my wife more than anyone else but we still, even after twenty-three years of marriage, have things that we do not see eye to eye on. We have learned to compromise for the sake of peace and our mutual well-being. We never compromise on principle, but we do compromise as it relates to methodology. Most people do not disagree on principle, but on methodology (the way that we do something).

Most all parents agree on the fact that their children must be disciplined. How, when, and to what degree become areas of conflict at times. We must learn to compromise and find ground that both parties can stand on together and be happy. We must realize it is things concerning methodology that the enemy will come to bring offense over in the church.

Let's take the area of praise and worship. The majority of believers will agree that we should praise and worship the Lord. Yet, at what volume should the music be? What should the song selection be? Who is going to sing on the worship team? These are the things that begin to cause people to get offended and ultimately uproot themselves.

There are believers that actually get upset over the volume level of the music. Usually, it is because it is too loud. However, there are some who think that it is not loud enough. If it is too loud for you, then sit more towards the rear of the building. If it is too soft, then sit closer to the front. Just do not allow it to become a point of contention and allow an offense to be taken.

Those who take an offense and leave the church over such things are immature. Once again, they are declaring to everyone with their actions that they are more important than anyone else. The church should revolve around them and their personal preferences. God help them to grow up and get potty-trained.

Jesus commanded us to be reconciled to our brother if we are offended. He did not say to leave the church offended and angry. In most situations where there has been an actual violation against another person, things can be worked out and reconciliation can result. It does require both parties to be mature enough to admit their mistakes and "kiss and make up."

Holding onto an offense will only cause us to continue to experience the hurt. We will look at everyone through tinted glasses. Anything that happens to us, that is remotely similar to the experience that offended and hurt us, will reopen the wound once again. The truth is we will never get healed of the wound until we get over the offense. We all need to get over it and get healed!

> A brother offended is harder to win than a strong city,
> and contentions are like the bars of a castle.
> —PROVERBS 18:19

The writer of Proverbs declares that being offended and having contentions in our life is like a prison. If we uproot ourselves because of offense and contention, there is nowhere for us to go other than spiritual prison. In prison there is no freedom. In prison you are locked up. Prison is a place of bondage and captivity.

We have a choice of where we are going to live. We can allow offense to rule our lives and end up in the spiritual prison. We can allow the love of God to rule our lives, get planted, and live a fruitful life in the house of the Lord. What choice are you going to make? I trust you will make the right choice by releasing any offense that you may be carrying and get planted in the house of the Lord.

He that is possessed with a prejudice is possessed with a
devil, and one of the worst kinds of devils, for it shuts out
the truth, and often leads to ruinous error.

—TRYON EDWARDS,
GREAT, GREAT-GRANDSON OF JONATHAN EDWARDS

Chapter 14

THE ENEMY CALLED PREJUDICE

*P*REJUDICE IS DEFINED as an inclination for or against that inhibits impartial and correct judgment. There are many different kinds of prejudices people operate with today. These prejudices negatively affect the lives of others and are many times destructive in nature. Ungodly prejudices will cause believers to be planted incorrectly.

The prejudice that most of us are familiar with more than any other is the issue of racial prejudice. This is a prejudice that judges someone based solely on the color of his or her skin or national heritage. It is a prejudice that has been in the world since sin entered the world.

Racial prejudice has been in the church since its inception. It was present in the early church. (See Galatians 2:11–13.) It brings division into the body and causes believers that God has

189

called to function together to be disjointed.

All races and nationalities have been guilty of racial prejudice. There are no innocent races or nationalities. All have, to one degree or another, been responsible for perpetuating it.

This does not mean that everyone in every race has been guilty. Rather, there is no race that has not had their share of people who were or are racially prejudiced.

We must realize this is an enemy of the Church and believers must get delivered from any prejudices they may have in this area. This type of prejudice is not of God and is sinful. It also reveals the lack of maturity in the person who practices it.

There are many wonderful books that have been written that deal with this type of prejudice and racial reconciliation in an elaborated manner. The church is making great strides in these areas. There are still things that need to be done and ground that must be covered. However, we can be thankful to God for the progress that has been made and continue to grow in the grace of God.

The area of racial prejudice is one that the vast majority of believers realize is wrong and sinful. Yet, there are many other prejudices active in the church which little is ever said about. Many times, these areas go unnoticed. These are the areas that I want to primarily focus on in this chapter.

There are hidden prejudices active in the church today. Little is said for the fear of offending someone who participates in these kinds of prejudices. Sometimes things are not said because it goes unrecognized.

These prejudices become like untreated cancer that cause all sorts of other spiritual ailments within the lives of believers. I want to shine the light on some of these and expose them so healing and deliverance can come.

The first one is that of financial prejudice. This prejudice negatively affects those in all financial spectrums. Rich and poor have been affected by this one.

Financial prejudice causes people to judge others entirely by their financial status. The worth and value of others is based solely upon their financial position. Again, people on both ends of the financial spectrum and those in the middle have been influenced by this prejudice. Let me start with those who are blessed to the greater degree and at the top of the financial spectrum.

> Command those who are rich in this present age not to be haughty, nor to trust in uncertain riches but in the living God, who gives us richly all things to enjoy. Let them do good, that they be rich in good works, ready to give, willing to share, storing up for themselves a good foundation for the time to come, that they may lay hold on eternal life.
> —1 TIMOTHY 6:17–19

Notice that Paul says for those who have money and wealth "not to be haughty." Other words for haughty are proud, arrogant, conceited, and high-minded. God commands those who have an abundance of money not to have an exalted opinion concerning themselves. They are not to think their value in the church is determined by their bank account.

You may be asking, "How does this relate to being planted?" I am glad that you are curious to find the answer.

My wife and I now have over twenty-three years of full-time ministry experience. We have seen people come and go. We have seen rich and poor fall into the ditch of financial prejudice and not even realize it.

We have learned, because of things we have seen, observed, and experienced, that this prejudice is deceptive and will cause believers to not be planted. It is important that we deal with this. This financial prejudice manifests in several different ways that are destructive to the people of God.

One of the primary ways that it negatively influences the church

PLANTED

is through ungodly control. Many times, those who are financially blessed feel as though they should have a greater voice in the financial matters of the church regardless of their spiritual maturity level. They begin to feel that because they are giving more than others, it automatically entitles them to tell the pastor where and when money should be spent.

Many times these same people, when their advice is not heeded, take their marbles and go somewhere else. They uproot themselves from where God has ordained them to be because they cannot exert control. They are upset with the pastor because they view themselves as the embodiment of financial wisdom and their wonderful advice has not been followed.

The truth is many of these people are spiritual babies who are accustomed to having everything their way. They throw a tantrum if something is not done to their liking. They break covenant with those whom God has joined them after unsuccessfully trying to use their money to control the relationship.

My friend, this is sinful and devilish behavior. It is carnality on steroids. The attempt to use what God has blessed us with to manipulate and control those in spiritual authority is wrong. Those who try to manipulate and control through their money are guilty of the sin of trusting in riches. They have put their confidence in money and made it their strength.

We must realize that financial abundance does not automatically entitle anyone to a position, title, or special place in the church. Although, it does give them the opportunity to be a blessing to the kingdom of God and others.

Another way that this financial prejudice manifests is through the despising of spiritual authority. It causes those who are financially blessed to begin to feel and take action that refuses the counsel of their local church pastor. They begin to believe that because they have more money, they are therefore smarter.

The line of thinking is this: "I make more money than you, so I

192

am more successful. Since I am more successful, you cannot counsel me." This type of thinking is wrong. If it were accurate, the
richest men in America would be unable to receive counsel from
anyone. They would be spiritually void—which is true of many
because of their financial prejudice.

Business success does not exclude anyone from receiving from
his or her local church pastor. Neither does it exclude them from
the responsibility and command of being planted in a local church.
Regardless of our success, we never "outgrow" the local church.

This is the attitude that Paul was addressing. It was the attitude
of pride and arrogance. To say that our success excludes us from the
biblical commands of being planted is prideful along with deceptive.
At the root of most pride there is some form of deception.

To say that money and success make us better than the local
church is to discredit what God has ordained to be in the earth. It
devalues the local church to the place that our personal success and
bank accounts are greater than God's house.

This type of thinking leads some to believe they no longer need
the local church. They begin to think they are in some way exempt
from attending services because they have arrived.

For these believers, the premise they operate from is that the
church is only there to help them achieve success. Once success
is achieved, the local church has no more purpose in their lives. I
will concede that God has designed the local church to be a place
where our faith is strengthened and thereby we are made successful. However, this is only one of the many reasons we should be in
the house of the Lord.

We must realize this type of thinking is the seed of deception. It
allows the enemy to cause us to be uprooted from the local church
that God has ordained for us. It will cause us to wander around in
the wilderness being unconnected to the life source of the local
church. Ultimately, that path leads to destruction in our family
and finances.

On the other side of the financial spectrum is the financial prejudice exercised by those who have little. This financial prejudice is also manifested in several ways. One of the primary ways is by despising those who are prosperous.

There is an epidemic in this nation today called "class warfare." It pits those who do not have against those who do. The doctrine it imposes is that the reason you do not have anything is because of those who do. It blames those who are prosperous for the failures of those who are less fortunate.

The roots of this indoctrination are found in blame shifting and envy. Blame shifting began at the fall of man. When Adam fell, he immediately began to blame shift. When confronted by God, Adam blamed the only two intelligible beings he knew. He said, "The woman that You gave me." Adam blamed God and the woman.

Obviously, Adam did not want to take responsibility for anything that had transpired. It seems as though not much has changed in six thousand years. Man still wants to blame others when he finds himself in a situation that is difficult.

We must understand that despising what we desire will only repel it in our lives. The disdaining of those who are prosperous will only result in poverty in our own lives. Hating others for having what we want is nothing other than envy and covetousness.

We must learn to rejoice when we see others prospered. Paul spoke of this.

> And if one member suffers, all the members suffer with it; or if one member is honored, all the members rejoice with it.
>
> —1 CORINTHIANS 12:26

When we see our brother or sister honored, we should be delighted. Remember this: Whatever you celebrate, you will *become*. If you will celebrate prosperity in the lives of others, you will attract prosperity. If you despise prosperity in the lives of others, you will repel prosperity. The choice is yours. You can either attract prosperity or repel it. Attracting it is much better, so learn to celebrate when you see others blessed.

Believers who continue with this type of financial prejudice will ultimately become bitter. They will disconnect themselves from the local church where God has them planted. They usually leave with the accusation that no one cares for them or their plight.

They live as victims rather than victors; conquered rather than conquerors; whiners rather than winners; and rejected rather than resourceful. We see these type people on television talk shows. They have been taken advantage of by everybody, their brother, and their dog. What a miserable life!

The good news is that you do not have to live that way. You can make a decision to let go of your prejudice and hurt, and become healed, delivered, and set free. This will result in God's abundance being manifested in your life.

Another way that this financial prejudice is manifested is by making those who are less prosperous feel of lesser value to the church. This is a lie of the enemy that causes people to uproot themselves.

There is a desire within all humanity to be needed. No one wants to feel unnecessary. Everyone needs a purpose for his or her life. Our purpose usually involves the fulfilling of some need in the human race.

People get married because they love and need one another. God told Adam in the beginning that he (Adam) needed someone. So God made Eve for him and she was the fulfillment of Adam's need. He needed her for procreation. He needed her for fellowship. He needed her for companionship. Eve found her fulfillment in meeting Adam's need. He found fulfillment in meeting Eve's need.

Since the dawn of creation, everyone has desired to be needed because God created man and woman to fulfill a need. When

PLANTED

someone feels unnecessary, it will cause them to begin to look for someone or someplace that will make them feel needed. If the enemy can get anyone to believe the lie that they are not needed in the church, he can then uproot them from the place where they are truly needed.

At the root of most of these types of feelings are issues of self-worth. Many people have their self-worth tied to their financial status. This happens with the rich and the poor. Either way, it is a mistake to tie our self-worth to our financial status.

Most of the time, those who begin to feel meaningless are those who are on the low end of the financial spectrum. The enemy uses their financial situation along with self-worth issues to alienate them from what will turn their situation around. The enemy causes them to feel unneeded and inferior. This results in them leaving the church where God has ordained them to be.

It is a tragedy that these people continue to wander around the wilderness and go around the mountain again and again. They go from place to place, but never feel a part or needed because of their prejudice and self-worth issues. The sad thing is it could be avoided, if they would merely let go of their prejudice and allow the Lord to come and heal them.

There is another prejudice that we see operating in the church. It is a deeply hidden one that few would ever admit to because it is easy to hide. It is known as educational prejudice.

It is a prejudice that judges and evaluates someone entirely on their educational achievement. Once again, just like financial prejudice, this affects those on both ends of the spectrum.

This prejudice manifests primarily in one of two ways. The first way is the disposition that causes one to disregard anyone who does not have numerous degrees listed before and after their name. The other way it manifests is the disposition that causes one to disregard anyone who sounds intelligent and well educated. Both are improper and will cause us to miss out on God's best for our lives.

Throughout the Bible we have evidenced that God used the educated and the uneducated. In the New Testament we have two very clear examples of this. Peter was a fisherman and was known in religious circles as being "uneducated and untrained" (Acts 4:13). Paul, on the other hand, was very educated in the Jewish theology and had a reputation of being a scholar. God used them both in tremendous ways.

It is interesting to point out that God sent Peter, the uneducated one, to the Jews who had great respect for education in Jewish law. Yet, Paul, the Jewish scholar, was sent to the Gentiles who did not care at all about Jewish law or religion.

I believe God did this intentionally. He was demonstrating that our ministry in the kingdom of God would not be determined by our education or the lack thereof. He sent the ignorant to the intelligent and the scholar to the illiterate.

Peter was described as "uneducated and untrained" (Acts 4:13). The original Greek word that is translated "untrained" is *idiotes*. It means "ignoramus" or "idiot." That is how Peter was known to be. Yet, it was his shadow that caused miracles and his sermon that won three thousand people to the Lord in one day.

> For you see your calling, brethren, that not many wise according to the flesh, not many mighty, not many noble, are called. But God has chosen the foolish things of the world to put to shame the wise, and God has chosen the weak things of the world to put to shame the things which are mighty; and the base things of the world and the things which are despised God has chosen, and the things which are not, to bring to nothing the things that are, that no flesh should glory in His presence.
>
> —1 CORINTHIANS 1:26–29

To judge someone based on their educational qualifications or the lack of it, is to limit how God can minister to us and through us. We must understand that God uses the foolish things to confound the wise. Paul refers to the preaching of the Gospel as foolishness to the natural mind.

> For the message of the cross is foolishness to those who are perishing, but to us who are being saved it is the power of God.
>
> —1 CORINTHIANS 1:18

It does not make sense how the red blood of Jesus can be applied to a black sinful heart and make it white as snow. That confounds the natural mind of men. We must understand that the foundation of Christianity is based upon the truth that the intellectual mind has great difficulty receiving. Yet, there are those in the body of Christ who idolize educational achievement to the point that it produces a prejudice in their lives. This is not right and must be corrected.

Understand that I am in no way saying that we should despise education. I believe educational accomplishment is a wonderful thing. It is a noble achievement. However, if it determines our outlook on others in the body of Christ, we need to examine ourselves.

At the same time, we need to know that there is not a premium on ignorance. It is not the prerequisite to being used by God. God uses the educated and the uneducated. What is important is that we not allow either to affect the way we view others in the body of Christ, particular those who God has placed in authority within our lives.

It is ironic that Peter, known as ignorant and uneducated, was headquartered in Jerusalem. He was sent to minister to those who were educated in Judaism. He had no degree from rabbinical school. His only accolade was that he had been with Jesus.

Some of the most powerful men in the body of Christ have had little formal Bible education. They have studied intently on their own. They have spent hours on their faces before God, receiving fresh revelation. They have a call and anointing to expound the Word of God in ways that no other would be able to do. Having educational prejudices will cut you off from those who have a divine revelation yet lack an educational degree to your satisfaction.

Those who practice this type of prejudice will usually only associate with those who are on their intellectual level, whatever it may be. They either feel superior or inferior to those who are outside their circles. This ultimately causes sectarianism in the church. It brings division and discord that ultimately leads to different ones leaving the church because of exclusionism. This is wrong behavior and believing. If this is the type premise you operate your life from, ask the Lord to forgive you and extend His grace towards you so you can walk free of this damaging disposition.

Another prejudice that I will mention briefly is that of geographical prejudice. This prejudice judges others based on where they are from or the accent with which they speak. It is a prejudice that makes assumptions about another's disposition based entirely on where they grew up or what region of the world they live in.

In the United States there are still some people, even born again believers, who make incorrect assumptions concerning others. Those from the northern United States have been rudely referred to as "Yankees." They are considered to be discourteous, obnoxious, arrogant, and unfeeling. Although there may be some from the northern United States that behave in that manner, not all do.

On the other hand, there are some who will make incorrect assumptions concerning those who were born and raised in the southern United States. They have been rudely referred to as "rednecks." Many times, they are even considered racists based on the accent they possess in speaking. Sometimes, they are presumed to be ignorant "hicks." Although, there may be some from the southern United States that behave in this manner, not all do. These false presumptions are based entirely on geographical prejudices. This prejudice is very closely related to racial prejudice. It acts and responds in very similar ways. It is an ungodly prejudice that must be eradicated in the body of Christ. We must not make assumptions about our fellow member of the body of Christ based on where they originated.

Those who function with this prejudice, like other prejudices, exclude different members of the church from their circles. This has a damaging affect on others as well as themselves. My friend, if God wants to use someone with a little different manner of speech then yourself to minister a life giving word to you, then do not get upset about the vessel He is using. We all have unique characteristics about our speech and mannerisms. We cannot allow things such as this to become a roadblock within our lives and cut us off from those God has strategically placed within our lives.

The last prejudice that I want to discuss briefly is that of gender prejudice. There are some in the body of Christ today that cannot receive ministry from anyone who is not of the male gender. They somehow believe that God's prerequisite for someone to minister in the church is that they are a man (not a woman).

> There is neither Jew nor Greek, there is neither slave nor free, there is neither male nor female; for you are all one in Christ Jesus.
>
> —GALATIANS 3:28

We must understand that God is not examining someone's physical body to see if they are male or female before He places His call or anointing on them. A physical examination by the Father is not the prerequisite for functioning in ministry.

There seems to be some misunderstanding of a few scriptures written that cause some to exclude women from any opportunity to minister or hold an office in the body of Christ. There are some wonderful books written that expel these misunderstandings. For an in depth examination of this subject, I would suggest you reading the book *Redefining the Role of Women in the Church* by Dr. Jim Davis.

My wife, Stacey, and I pastor together. We are one. She carries the same authority that I have. She shares some of the same responsibilities that I possess. We work together.

I believe the greatest ministry team that God has ever placed together is husband and wife. This is God's pattern that began at creation. God did not create another man for Adam. He created a woman. He created a wife for Adam. She was to be his helper.

Helpers share the responsibilities of those they are helping. Helpers do the same things as those they are helping. Helpers do not do "their own thing." They participate with those they are helping.

There are numerous places throughout the Bible that God used women in mighty and powerful ways. Women were the first to preach the Gospel. (See John 20:18.) To say that God has disallowed women from participating in church ministry (including fivefold ministry) is to say that God is a sexist. I assure you that He is not.

A particular brother in our church was sharing how he had invited someone in the community to come and visit our church. They replied to him, "As long as there is a woman's name on the front of that building, I'll never go there." On the front of our building it says, "Pastors: Robert and Stacey Gay." This man's gender prejudice will be a roadblock in his life that will keep him from receiving God's best.

Some may say, "You just don't understand; that's just the way it is and people are going to judge others based on these things." I do understand that many people are this way, but it does not make it right. I understand that people lie, but it does not make it right. I understand that people commit adultery, but it does not make it right. I understand that people get divorced because they get tired of each other, but it does not make it right.

Since when should we as believers just accept things as they are when we know they are wrong? God has called us to be agents of change in the earth. We are called to be salt and light. It is time for us to season and let our light shine.

Prejudices in the church today will cause us to become uprooted. They will cause us to see the world through "tinted glasses." Prejudices negatively affect our ability to receive from the Lord. They cause us to limit how God can minister to us.

We must learn to embrace God's ministers whether they are rich or poor, educated or not educated, male or female, and regardless of the color of their skin or where they were born and raised. God desires to use everyone who is planted in His house.

As we allow God to deliver us from any prejudice in our lives, it will enable us to receive from the Lord to a greater degree. God is faithful and will come and heal us if we will only call on Him.

CONCLUSION

E HAVE EXAMINED numerous Scriptures that have articulated the importance of being planted in the house of the Lord. We have seen the importance God places on us being intricately connected to a local church.

Those who become planted in the house of the Lord will see God's blessing within their lives. God will bring prosperity and blessing upon our families as we begin to serve the Lord together. The promise to all who are planted is that there will be breakthrough in their lives. As we go to the place that the Lord has chosen for us, we will see the favor of God released within our lives.

It is important that we not allow extracurricular activities to take priority over the house of the Lord. God has designed the local church to be a life-source for our families. As we go there and give there, there will be spiritual food for us to eat. We will be fed by the hand of the Lord, as we are faithful to be in His house. It is there that He will prepare a table before us and our cup will overflow.

We must understand that God is the Master Gardener. He takes care of the plants that are planted in His garden. He will nourish and cultivate every plant. God will cause us to grow as we allow ourselves to be planted. It is important to remain where God has planted us.

God originated the principles of the seed. Everything in the kingdom of God works from the principles that we see in the seed. That which is least, once it is sown, becomes greater than all. Regardless of how small you may think you are, being planted will cause great growth to come into your life. The principle of the seed will come alive in our lives as we allow ourselves to be planted in the house of the Lord.

The law of sowing and reaping does not only apply to the area of financial giving, but is relevant in every area of our life. As we allow ourselves to be sown into the local church, we will reap a harvest from the same. The greater the planting, the greater the reaping.

God desires for us to be like a tree planted by the rivers of water. He wants our roots to go down deep. The deeper the roots, the greater the fruit.

As our roots are strengthened, we will become those who are immoveable. It is deep roots that will bring stability within our lives. The shaking that comes will only be used to reveal the fruit. We will be those who are consistent in our Christian walk and fruit production. We will bring forth fruit in our season.

Fruit is the byproduct of being planted in fertile soil. God is glorified when we bear fruit. Fruitfulness pleases the heart of the Father, as others are able to partake of the fruit He intended for us to bear.

As we bear fruit, God will come to prune us. He will cut back branches in certain seasons so we will bear greater fruit. It is important that we not run from the pruning process. When God begins to deal with issues in our lives, we must not be those who "jump and run," nor can we despise the one God uses to prune us. Pruning is a good thing that will enable us to grow and mature.

We are commanded in the Word of God to not forsake the assembling of ourselves together. We are told to gather together for the purpose of encouraging and edifying one another. The Father has given us an invitation to come to His house. It is important that we place great value on the invitation and most of all the one who is inviting. Just as it was the habit of Jesus and Paul to attend the gathering of the believers, we must also make it our habit.

God told us to "Remember the Sabbath Day" (Exod. 20:8). We should give honor to and consecrate a day of the week to come together with the other members of our local church and be spiritually refreshed. God instituted the Sabbath Day to be a day of rest and spiritual refreshing and it still relevant for New Testament believers today.

Every believer should be a member of a local church. God not only wants our name registered and on the roll in heaven, but also here on earth. Church membership is important to God, so it should be important to us. Local church membership is a statement of our faith, commitment, and love for the Body of Christ.

At the time of creation, God told Adam that it was not good for him to be alone. Man has been created to be interdependent. We cannot spiritually survive without others in the Church. We need the ministry of our fellow members to enable us to be complete in Christ. It is the banana that gets separated from the bunch that gets peeled and eaten.

Every Christian has a gift that has been given to them. God has designed our giftings to be activated, developed, and exercised in the local church. Since we have received gifts, we are commanded to minister our gifts to one another. As we do, we become good stewards of the grace that God has bestowed upon our lives.

Gifts are given and are not on loan. God expects us to use what we have received. We will either use it or lose it. As we are faithful with what we have been given, God will give us more.

To truly be planted, we must also give of our finances. God commands us to bring the tithe to the house of the Lord for the support of the ministry that is conducted there. As we are obedient to God's command, we will see the abundance of heaven come into our lives.

There are some in the body of Christ that are not planted because of offense they harbor. It is important that we get over our offense and get on with what God has commissioned us to do. Jesus commanded us to be reconciled to our brother, not leave the church angry.

Offense is the greatest enemy that keeps Christians from getting planted and staying planted. By the grace of God, we will arise and overcome. We cannot afford to let our past keep us from fulfilling our future. We must let go of the hurts and disappointments of yesterday and embrace the healing and destiny that God has for us today.

God has called us to be His servants. We serve Him by serving others. The apostle John said, "he who does not love (serve) his brother whom he has seen, how can he love (serve) God whom he has not seen" (1 John 4:20). We are called to serve one another. We must make a commitment to serve in the house of the Lord. That commitment will bring forth the blessing of God in our lives and the lives of others.

God has called the church to be the salt of the earth and the light of the world. We, of all people, must demonstrate the absence of prejudices. Any prejudice, whether it is racial, financial, educational, geographical, or gender, will negatively affect our lives. It will keep us from receiving God's best. It will cause our light to be dim and our salt to lose its flavor.

We must make a quality decision to get somewhere and plant it. Let us allow God to work on us, in us, and through us. The apostle

Paul said, "He who has begun a good work in you will complete it until the day of Jesus Christ" (Phil. 1:6).

My prayer for you is that you will arise to fulfill your destiny and accomplish the will of God. His destiny and will for your life involves, to some degree or another, the local church. Let us all become planted, rooted, and established in the house of the Lord.

For more information on available products from Robert Gay or for ministry scheduling, contact us at:

Robert L. Gay
High Praise Worship Center
7124 E. Hwy. 22
Panama City, FL 32404

Phone: (850) 874-9745
Fax: (850) 874-9744

E-Mail: highpraise@knology.net
Web Address: www.hipraz.com

NOTES

Chapter 8
WHAT IT MEANS TO BE PLANTED

1. See www.eadshome.com/TheodoreRoosevelt.htm, accessed November 18, 2004.

Chapter 9
REMEMBER THE SABBATH DAY

1. *Adam Clarke's Commentary*, Electronic Database. Copyright (c) 1996 by Biblesoft.

2. *Barnes' Notes,* Electronic Database. Copyright (c) 1997 by Biblesoft.

3. *Jamieson, Fausset, and Brown Commentary,* Electronic Database. Copyright (c) 1997 by Biblesoft.

4. *Matthew Henry's Commentary on the Whole Bible,* New Modern Edition, Electronic Database. Copyright (c) 1991 by Hendrickson Publishers, Inc.

5. Ibid.

Chapter 11
YOU HAVE SOMETHING TO GIVE

1. Bill Hamon, *The Eternal Church* (n.p.: Destiny Image Publishers, 1981).

Chapter 14
THE ENEMY CALLED PREJUDICE

1. See www.thinkexist.com, accessed November 18, 2004.